SCIENCE
IS
AWESOME!

101 INCREDIBLE THINGS EVERY KID SHOULD KNOW

LISA REGAN

ARCTURUS

ARCTURUS

This edition published in 2018 by Arcturus Publishing Limited
26/27 Bickels Yard, 151–153 Bermondsey Street,
London SE1 3HA

All images from Shutterstock except p25(t) Jerry Pike; p47 Nasa; p49(t)
aphotostory / Shutterstock.com; p67 Wellcome Library; p77(t) Gilles
Paire / Shutterstock.com; p81(b) Wellcome Library; p83 Stuart Elflett
/ Shutterstock.com; p90 Nasa; p96 Byelikova Oksana / Shutterstock.
com; p121(b) homydesign / Shutterstock.com; p123(t) Rainer Herhaus /
Shutterstock.com; p124 Nasa / Shutterstock; p125(b) Nasa.

Written by Lisa Regan
Designed by Trudi Webb

ISBN: 978-1-78599-872-0
CH004677NT
Supplier 26, Date 0118, Print run 6618

Printed in China

Contents

FACT 1

ONE QUARTER OF ALL ANIMALS ARE BEETLES

That's right: one of every four living creatures is a beetle. There are at least 300,000 known types, more than any other animal, and they live in every habitat except the ocean.

THE SMALLEST BEETLE CAN ONLY BE SEEN USING A MICROSCOPE.

Sorting them out

There are a vast number of different creatures living on this planet, with new ones being discovered all the time. Scientists arrange and describe them according to their similarities and differences. Beetles are grouped with other insects, which all have six legs and three body parts. Bees, ants, butterflies, and flies are all in the insect group.

Keep it in the family

All animals belong to the same large group, known as a **kingdom**. This is divided into smaller groups, gradually separating the animals into **classes** such as insect, bird, reptile, or mammal. Classes are then divided into **orders** and **families**, so that similar creatures such as monkeys are grouped with each other. Monkeys are mammals of the order primates, which is the same order that people belong to.

Marmosets, tamarins, baboons, and mandrills are all monkeys.

FUNGI LOOK LIKE PLANTS, BUT HAVE MORE IN COMMON WITH THE ANIMAL KINGDOM.

Different kingdoms

Not all living things are animals. The other kingdoms include plantae (all green plants, from moss to daisies to giant sequoia trees) and fungi (mushrooms and toadstools). Bacteria and amoebas are in their own different kingdoms.

Homo sapiens, pleased to meet you.

The name game

Centuries ago, botanists (who study plants) and zoologists (who study animals) voyaged around the world, making new discoveries all the time. They needed a way to organize and name all their findings. In the 1750s, Swedish scientist Carl Linnaeus devised a new system, which was so good it is still used today. His taxonomic system arranges things into sensible groups, and gives them two-part names so that all scientists know they are talking about the same creatures.

Carl Linnaeus
1707–1778

FACT 2

SOME JELLYFISH ARE IMMORTAL

Like frogs and butterflies, jellyfish go through different stages before they become adults. Some species can revert back to their baby form, so they never really die.

Again and again

A jellyfish starts life as an egg, which attaches itself to the ocean floor. It turns into a polyp with tentacles, like a microscopic sea anemone. This polyp feeds and grows until it is ready to turn into several adults and move around. Each one is a clone (identical copy) of the others. Some jellyfish live for a few months; others live for many years. When the immortal jellyfish (scientific name *Turritopsis dohrnii*) gets old or injured, it can change from its adult form back to the polyp stage, repeating the cycle over and over again. If it doesn't get eaten, it can theoretically live forever!

JELLYFISH ARE ABOUT 95% WATER; THAT'S WHY THEY TURN INTO A BLOB WHEN THEY'RE OUT OF WATER.

Crazy creatures

A grown-up jellyfish is called a medusa, and that's what you see when you visit the coast. Jellyfish have no brain, no heart, no bones, and no blood. They can barely swim, but float using ocean currents. However, they do have stinging tentacles to trap their food.

Sea anemones have venom-filled tentacles to catch prey.

Spineless stingers

Jellyfish are part of the animal kingdom, and belong to the group called Cnidaria. This includes other stinging sea creatures such as anemones, sea pens, and corals. They are closely related to comb jellies, which don't have stinging tentacles. All of them are **invertebrates**: animals without a spine (backbone).

Other invertebrates

Around 97% of the world's creatures don't have a backbone. Many of them have a hard shell on the outside (an exoskeleton) to protect their body parts. They are incredibly successful at surviving in all sorts of habitats, from deep oceans to dry deserts. Spiders, scorpions, starfish, sea slugs, worms, insects, and crabs are all invertebrates.

CRABS CAN WALK IN ANY DIRECTION, BUT RUN SIDEWAYS IF THEY NEED TO MOVE QUICKLY.

FACT 3
AN OCTOPUS HAS THREE HEARTS

A mammal like you has one heart, but that's not enough for the octopus. It has a heart to move blood around its body, and two extra hearts to pump blood to its gills (see page 10).

A squash and a squeeze

An octopus also has more limbs than most animals. Its eight arms have suckers on them to help it move and grasp things, for sensing, and for catching its food. Octopuses have virtually no hard body parts, so can squeeze through tiny gaps. The only firm part is a beak, in the middle of the body, used for crushing and eating shellfish.

OCTOPUS PUPILS ROTATE TO STAY HORIZONTAL NO MATTER WHICH WAY UP THE OCTOPUS TURNS.

The heart of the matter

The heart is a muscle that pumps blood around the body. The blood carries vital nutrients, and removes unwanted products like carbon dioxide. Blood flows through separate sections of the heart, depending on whether or not it is carrying oxygen. A human heart has four sections, or **chambers**, but not all creatures work like this. A worm has five hearts to squeeze blood around its body. An insect's heart is like a tube along its back.

Octopuses are extremely good at blending in with their surroundings.

Yes, I know my tail is blue. I'm a blue-tailed skink.

A SKINK CAN GROW A NEW TAIL IN THREE TO FOUR MONTHS, BUT THE NEW TAIL HAS NO BONES IN IT.

On the defensive

A threatened octopus has several ways to defend itself. Its skin changes shade, both for camouflage and to show that it is angry. It can squirt out a cloud of ink to confuse its predator while it makes its escape. It can also cast off part of an arm, which carries on wiggling to tempt the predator. The octopus can grow back a new bit to replace the lost section. This is called **regeneration**.

Growing again

Several creatures can lose a body part and grow a new one. Some starfish can divide in two, with each half becoming a new starfish. One type of starfish can regenerate its whole body from a single arm! Many lizards, including geckos and skinks, can simply drop their tail if they get caught, and later grow a new one.

SOME FISH CAN LIVE ON LAND

Not all fish live in the water all of the time. Some species, such as the mudskipper and leaping blenny, can move onto land for hours at a time.

A freaky fish

Most fish breathe underwater. They have flaps called gills at each side of their neck. A fish takes in water through its mouth and pushes it out through the gills, where oxygen is gathered and sent around its body. The mudskipper, however, can eat and breed on land. It carries pockets of water so it can breathe, just as a person uses scuba tanks to survive underwater. It even uses its pectoral (side) fins like legs, so it can walk instead of swim.

A MUDSKIPPER CAN MOVE EACH OF ITS EYES IN A DIFFERENT DIRECTION.

Ah, fresh air!

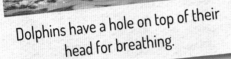

Dolphins have a hole on top of their head for breathing.

Take a deep breath

All animals need to breathe oxygen. The body uses this oxygen to help turn food into fuel, for energy. Mammals take in air through their mouth and nose, and it travels into the lungs where the oxygen is transferred into the blood stream. Even aquatic mammals, such as dolphins and seals, need to come to the water's surface to breathe.

Another approach

Insects don't breathe through gills, or their mouth. They don't even have lungs. Instead, they have rows of tiny holes called **spiracles** along their body. These are connected to air tubes that carry oxygen to where it is needed.

How many gills?

Fish can be roughly divided into two types: bony (like cod, perch, and piranha) or cartilaginous (sharks and rays). Bony fish, as you would expect, have a skeleton made of bone. They have just one gill slit on each side. The skeleton of a shark or ray is made of cartilage, the same as the gristly lower part of your nose. These fish have several gills; most sharks have five slits on each side.

FACT 5

WOOD FROGS FREEZE IN WINTER

Animals cope with the cold in all sorts of ways. Wood frogs allow their body to freeze, so much that they become hard and crunchy! Then they simply thaw out in the spring.

FACT 6

Squirrels bury food so they don't starve in winter. They can remember the hiding places of 10,000 nuts.

Facing the freeze

Some animals migrate to warmer places for the winter, while others hibernate. But this special frog stays in its natural habitat, settles down to weather the storm, and simply lets its skin and blood freeze when the temperature drops. Unlike humans, which suffer from frostbite if their body parts get too cold, the frog produces a sugary substance in its cells, which stops the cold from damaging them.

THE WOOD FROG'S HEART STOPS BEATING WHILE IT IS FROZEN.

Is it bedtime yet?

Hedgehogs go into a kind of deep sleep called hibernation.

Deep sleep

Some animals sleep the whole way through the cold season. They feed as much as they can while food is available, and then settle into their burrow or nest. While they sleep, their body temperature drops, their breathing and heartbeat get slower, and their body conserves energy. Ground squirrels, tortoises, hedgehogs, and many frogs and toads sleep and wake through winter, while some bears sleep nonstop for months.

Split personality

Frogs are amphibians. That means they start life as water dwellers, and as they grow they spend more time on land. Toads, newts, salamanders, and blindworms are also amphibians.

FACT 7

The paradoxical frog has tadpoles four times bigger than the adults.

The circle of life

Amphibians have a very distinctive life cycle. They begin as eggs, or spawn, and hatch in the water. Tadpoles emerge, which look nothing like their parents. They are small blobs with a tail for swimming and gills for breathing. Gradually, they grow legs and the tail disappears. They no longer breathe through their gills, and can move around on land.

13

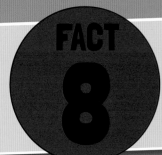

FACT 8
UNBORN SAND TIGER SHARKS ARE CANNIBALS

It's survival of the fittest from the very beginning. The biggest, healthiest sand tiger shark babies eat their brothers and sisters before they're even born!

A baby with bite

Sand tiger sharks start life as eggs inside their mother. When the first eggs hatch, the tiny sharks eat the other eggs. Then the two biggest shark pups eat all of the other babies before they are born. Scientists studying pregnant sand tiger sharks have even had their fingers bitten by the babies inside their mother!

FACT 9
Sharks have been on Earth for over 400 million years; they're older than dinosaurs.

A SHARK'S SKIN IS COVERED IN SCALES. IT FEELS ROUGH IF YOU STROKE IT THE WRONG WAY.

Being born

Generally speaking, reptiles, fish (including sharks), amphibians, and birds all lay eggs (see page 19). Fish often release thousands of tiny eggs into the water and leave them to fend for themselves. Many get eaten, but there are so many eggs that at least some of them survive and grow into adults. Some sharks do things differently, and hatch their eggs inside them so they emerge as bigger babies that have a greater chance of survival. They are known as **viviparous**.

Shark eggs have a leathery outside to protect the growing baby.

FACT 10

Some sharks go into a trance and stay perfectly still if you turn them upside down.

Shark attack!

Great white sharks are known to attack humans, but bull sharks and tiger sharks can be equally dangerous. Bull sharks don't need to live in salty seawater. They are specially adapted to survive in river water, so they can swim much closer to places where humans live, wash, and swim. Tiger sharks are aggressive and will eat just about anything. They have been found with all sorts of unexpected items in their stomach, including boots, pieces of cars and boats, and even a fur coat!

Gentle giant

There are over 400 species of shark, but not all of them are fearsome, razor-toothed monsters. The world's largest shark is the whale shark, but it won't bite you. It is a filter feeder, so it swims around with its huge mouth wide open to scoop up tiny creatures.

SNAKES CAN'T BLINK

A snake's eye has just one eyelid, which is see-through and fixed in place. It doesn't have movable eyelids to allow it to blink.

SNAKE SCALES ARE MADE OF KERATIN, THE SAME STUFF YOUR FINGERNAILS AND HAIR ARE MADE OF.

Oh my eyes!

A snake's eye is covered in clear scales to protect it. As a snake grows, it gets too big for its skin. It sheds the top layer of skin to reveal a new layer underneath. The eyelid, or eyecap, also comes off. It turns cloudy and blue, and the snake cannot see well until the shedding is finished.

THE SCALES ON A SNAKE'S BELLY ARE ROUGH, TO HELP IT GRIP.

Super senses

Most snakes have poor eyesight, so they rely on other senses to help them hunt. When a snake flicks out its tongue, it is collecting scents. It has a special organ in its mouth for understanding these smells. A snake's ears are hidden inside its head, and it also picks up vibrations in its jaw to hear things coming. Some snakes have an extra sense: they can tell when other creatures are near, using a heat-sensitive pit in their mouth.

Snakes have no sense of taste, but use their tongue for smelling.

Hey, man, it's cool being ectothermic.

On the attack

How does a creature with no arms or legs catch its food? Using venom or muscle-power, that's how. Constrictors wrap their coils around prey and squeeze until it can no longer breathe. Venomous snakes, such as vipers and cobras, inject deadly toxins using their hollow fangs.

Basking in the sun

Snakes are reptiles, a class of animals that have scales and are **ectothermic** (often called cold-blooded). They cannot control their body temperature from within, but have to lie in the Sun to warm up, or hide in the shade to cool down. This uses less energy, so they don't need to eat as much as birds and mammals. Crocodiles, alligators, tortoises, turtles, and lizards are all reptiles.

17

FACT 12

ONE BIRD'S BEAK IS LONGER THAN ITS BODY

Birds' beaks come in all shapes and sizes. The only bird with a beak longer than its body is the sword-billed hummingbird from South America.

Made to measure

A bird's beak is specially adapted to help it eat. Hummingbirds need a very long, thin beak to poke into flowers and reach the nectar that is their only food. They stick out their long tongue and lap up the sugary juice. Finches have a strong, short beak for cracking seeds, and a woodpecker's beak is like a chisel for breaking into trees. Birds of prey need a sharp, hooked beak, while the pelican has its own fishing pouch attached to its beak!

Just...a bit...further...

Specialist feeder

Hummingbirds are uniquely adapted to their special diet. They can hover alongside flowers, and are the only birds able to fly backward. They flap their wings around 50 times a second to stay aloft. Their long tongue has two grooves, like a W, and has tiny hairs on the end to collect nectar.

18

What makes a bird a bird?

Birds are in a scientific class of their own. All of them have a beak and wings, and are **endothermic** (warm-blooded). Birds are the only creatures alive today that have feathers. These may help them to fly, or attract a mate, or act as camouflage so they can hide. Feathers protect a bird's skin and trap heat to keep them warm.

A peacock shows off his magnificent feathers to attract a female.

FACT 13

Feathers, like scales, are made of keratin. Birds have both.

Flying high?

Although not all birds can fly, there are some that spend almost their whole life in the air. Swifts fly for months without landing, and albatrosses soar thousands of miles without even flapping their wings. Penguins can't fly, but use their wings as flippers for swimming. Ratites (ostriches, emus, and their relatives) are flightless but can run really fast.

Inside the egg

Female birds lay eggs with hard shells. Like the eggs of reptiles, they contain a yolk for the unborn baby to feed on, and a liquid to protect the growing creature. Reptile eggs can have a hard shell or a soft, leathery shell. Baby birds and reptiles have an egg tooth: an extra tooth or spike to help them break out from the inside. It falls off soon after hatching.

FACT 14

A BABY CAMEL IS BORN WITHOUT A HUMP

A camel's hump is full of fat. It acts as an emergency food supply in the desert. A baby camel's hump only grows when it begins to eat solid food.

Baby food

Camels are adapted to live in extreme conditions. They can walk for days without eating or drinking, living off the supplies in their hump. As they do so, the hump shrinks and droops to one side. When they eat and drink again, the hump is restored. Like all mammals, baby camels feed on their mother's milk. The milk contains all the goodness the baby needs to grow strong.

REMEMBER!
D IS FOR DROMEDARY (WITH ONE HUMP). B IS FOR BACTRIAN (WITH TWO HUMPS).

Growing up

Mammals give birth to live young, after the baby has developed in the womb. The babies usually look like miniature versions of their parents. Most mammals keep their babies with them and teach them how to survive, until they're ready to fend for themselves. They gradually wean them off milk and onto their adult food. Herbivores, like cows, eat only plants. Carnivores, like big cats, eat only meat. Omnivores, like bears and chimpanzees, eat a bit of everything.

Apes usually give birth to a single baby at a time.

Before they're born

Mammal babies spend weeks or months growing inside their mother. Rodents, such as rats, are born after two or three weeks. Humans develop for around nine months, and elephant mothers carry their baby for a year and three quarters!

FACT 15

A baby koala has to eat its mother's dung to get the bacteria needed to break down its adult diet of eucalyptus leaves.

TWO MAMMALS LAY EGGS: THE PLATYPUS AND THE ECHIDNA. THEY ARE CALLED MONOTREMES.

Put in a pocket

Marsupials are a special kind of mammal and are found mostly in Australasia. Their babies are born early, when they are too tiny to survive alone. They crawl into their mother's pouch where they continue to feed and grow.

PLANKTON CAN'T SWIM

Plankton are tiny animals and plants that live in water. Despite that, they cannot actually swim against a current. Even their name comes from the Greek for "drifter."

Eating to survive

Plankton may be microscopically small, but they are extremely important. They form part of a **food chain** that keeps all the world's creatures alive. All animals must eat. Some eat plants, and in turn are eaten by other animals. Shrimps and other small sea creatures eat plankton; small fish eat the shrimps; big fish eat the small fish; larger predators such as sea lions and dolphins eat the big fish.

Just call me Top Cat.

Life at the top

Some animals are large and dominant enough to avoid being eaten by any other creature. These animals are called **apex predators**. They can be found in most animal families: large eagles, crocodiles, boa constrictors, great white sharks, wolves, bears, and tigers are all at the top of their food chain.

THE WORLD'S BIGGEST ANIMAL, THE BLUE WHALE, FEEDS ON KRILL, SOME OF THE WORLD'S SMALLEST CREATURES.

Breaking the chain

A single change in a food chain can have enormous effects. The reduction in numbers, or the total extinction, of any species, will upset the balance. If an apex predator disappears, that will allow its prey to multiply in numbers. Those animals might eat all of the plant food, leaving none for other species. Take away a creature in the middle of the chain, and the animals above it will go hungry.

Specialist diets

Omnivores such as humans get their fuel from many different sources. Some animals have a much more restricted diet. The giant anteater feeds exclusively on ants and termites. It has developed a long tongue to lap them up from an anthill, and has no teeth as it doesn't need to chew its food. Vampire bats survive only on blood sucked from cattle and horses. Dung beetles get all the nutrition they need from other animals' dung!

23

FACT 17 CHICKENS ARE DINOSAURS!

Scientific studies have revealed that birds are the descendants of theropod dinosaurs. New fossils are being found all the time to support this theory.

Learning to fly

Theropods are a group of two-legged meat-eating dinosaurs that includes Tyrannosaurus rex, Velociraptor, and Allosaurus. **Paleontologists** (scientists who study fossils) think that these large dinosaurs shrank and changed over time to become birds. They developed into flying creatures, adapting to new environments such as treetops, and were able to survive the extinction that wiped out other dinosaurs 65 million years ago.

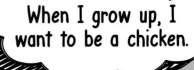

When I grow up, I want to be a chicken.

Cluck.

First feathers

Recent fossil finds show that some dinosaurs, such as Velociraptor, had feathers. They weren't used for flying, but did provide insulation, camouflage, and decoration in the same way they do for birds today. Fossils of dinosaur eggs and nests also show many similarities to those of birds. Some fossils even have preserved blood vessels which can be compared to the soft tissue of living birds.

Prehistoric science

Paleontologists use fossils to figure out what happened in the past. They can study life on Earth from millions of years ago. Thanks to them, we know what these extinct creatures ate, how fast they could run, and even how hard they could bite.

Ancient ancestors

Dinosaurs weren't the only animals to live way back in prehistory. They were joined by aquatic reptiles such as plesiosaurs and ichthyosaurs. Giant flying reptiles such as pterosaurs filled the skies. Although these creatures also became extinct 65 million years ago, other more familiar species survived. Snakes, crocodiles, lizards, sharks, bees, and dragonflies all had relatives that look very much like today's creatures. Early mammals existed, too, and evolved into the animals we see around us.

FACT 18
GIRAFFES SWORD FIGHT WITH THEIR NECKS

One of the most extraordinary scenes in nature is a fight between two male giraffes. Each enters into combat using its long neck as a weapon, head-butting the other male.

A GIRAFFE'S LEGS ARE TALLER THAN MOST GROWN HUMAN BEINGS.

Top of the list

Giraffes stick together in loose herds to look out for each other. Sometimes a male will fight another male to compete for a mating partner. One giraffe swings its long neck upward, using its hard head to ram into the other. They swap blows until a winner emerges. The fights are violent and hard-hitting, and a giraffe can be seriously injured.

You can't see me, right?

Deer mice have evolved dark or sandy fur, depending on where they live.

High hopes

A giraffe's long neck helps it in many ways. It can keep watch over great distances, and reach food high in the treetops that no other animal can get to. Giraffes graze for many hours each day, curling their extremely long, tough tongue around acacia branches to rip off the vegetation. The giraffe also has lots of thick saliva, to protect its mouth from the thorny trees. Each of the giraffe's special features has evolved over thousands of years to make them ideally suited to their habitat.

Nature at work

Over time, animals adapt to their environment in order to survive. They don't choose to; it happens naturally. A giraffe that can reach higher than other grazers will have a better chance of surviving, and its babies will carry on the successful characteristics. Gradually, the whole species will have longer necks and tougher tongues.

MORE THAN 120 ANIMAL SPECIES HAVE BEEN NAMED AFTER CHARLES DARWIN.

Scientific beliefs

Many scientists have studied the development of species. Charles Darwin spent years voyaging around the world and writing about the creatures he saw. He devised the theory of evolution to explain how nature selects the best characteristics for survival. His ideas got him into some big arguments, as they went against what the church of the time taught about the creation of the world.

Charles Darwin (1809–1882)

FACT 19 — BABIES HAVE MORE BONES THAN GROWN-UPS

Adult humans normally have 206 bones. Babies start life with more than 300. Some of these gradually fuse (join) together as they get older.

A head start

Humans are mammals, so they give birth to live young: babies, as we call them when they are mini-people! The baby starts life in the mother's womb and grows for around 40 weeks before it is born. Its head bone (cranium) is made of separate sections to allow it to squeeze more easily through the mother's body. A newborn baby has soft spots on its head that let the bony plates squash and move together.

BONES ARE CONSTANTLY WORN AWAY AND REBUILT.

FACT 20 — Your hands and feet contain over half your body's bones.

Bone on its own

Many of your bones are joined together by muscles or ligaments. The skull has eight cranial bones and another 14 facial bones that allow you to do things such as chew, hear, and laugh. The hyoid bone is not attached to your other bones, but is needed for speech. It is in just the right place in a human to allow us to talk. A lion's hyoid makes it roar, unlike a pet cat which can only purr.

A chimpanzee's hyoid is too high to allow it to speak properly.

FACT 21

Most people have a dozen pairs of ribs, but some people are born with an extra rib or pair of ribs by their neck.

Smile for the photographer!

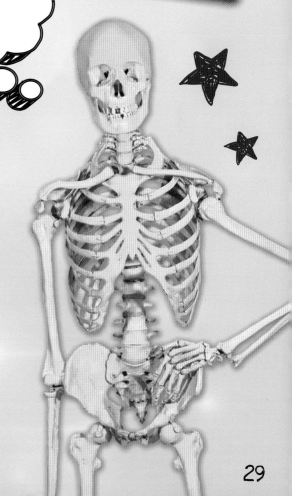

Bony bits

Bones start as cartilage (like a shark's skeleton, see page 11) and ossify (become real bone). A child's kneecaps are among the last body bits to turn to bone. Your body has different types of bone, including irregular bones which form your spine and flat bones in your chest and skull. Long bones are found in your arms and legs and have bumps at each end and bone marrow in the middle.

Multitasking

Bones are designed to protect your delicate vital organs such as your heart and brain. They provide a framework for your body so you can move. The bone marrow in long bones produces new blood cells: more than 200 billion every day!

29

FACT 22

BUTTERFLIES HAVE TASTE BUDS ON THEIR FEET

A person's five main senses are sight, hearing, taste, smell, and touch. You taste mainly with your tongue, but a butterfly has taste cells called receptors on its feet.

Mmm, tasty!

Your senses help you to function in the big wide world. They keep you safe. Without taste buds, you might eat food that is rotten or poisonous. Your taste buds tell you when you're eating something that your body needs, for example sweet things for energy and vegetables for vitamins. A butterfly uses its taste receptors to tell when it is on the right plant for feeding or laying its eggs.

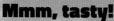

YOUR TASTEBUDS ARE REPLACED ABOUT EVERY TEN DAYS.

30

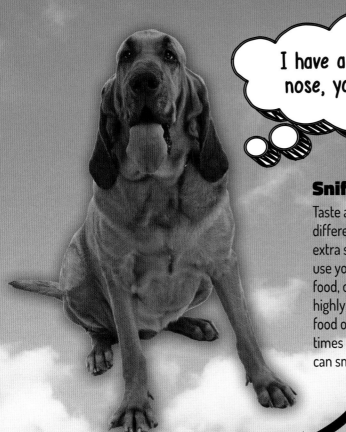

I have a superior nose, you know!

Sniffing it out

Taste and smell often work together. Foods send different chemicals up your nose to give you an extra sensation of how the food tastes. You also use your nose to detect danger: burning, rotting food, or poisonous gases. Many animals have a highly developed sense of smell to help them find food or avoid a predator. A bloodhound has 40 times more scent receptors than a human and can smell up to 10,000 times better!

IF YOU SMELL SOMETHING FOR TOO LONG, YOUR NOSE STOPS NOTICING IT.

Sound and vision

Hearing is important to people and animals. Sound waves are gathered and sent to the brain so we can hear people talking, jump away from an oncoming car, or run to the rescue when we hear a crash. People also rely heavily on their sight. Human eyes are positioned at the front of the head to allow us to judge distance, in contrast to prey animals such as horses and hens, whose side-facing eyes give them better peripheral vision (seeing a wide panorama around them).

More than a feeling

Your skin is your main touch receptor. It is also the body's largest organ. It contains millions of nerve endings which allow you to feel cold and heat, and pressure and pain. They send messages to your brain, which in turn instructs your muscles. It all happens without you even thinking about it.

FACT 23
MUSCLES CANNOT PUSH, THEY CAN ONLY PULL

Muscles are attached to your bones so you can move your body. A muscle works by contracting, or getting shorter, to pull the bone in the direction needed.

FACT 24
The longest muscle runs down the inner thigh to bend and twist the leg.

In and out

Each muscle can pull in only one direction, so they work in pairs. Think about bending your arm at the elbow. Your biceps muscle (at the top front of your arm) contracts and pulls up your lower arm. To straighten your arm again, the triceps muscle (underneath the biceps) pulls in the opposite direction. When one muscle is contracted, its opposite muscle is relaxed. These kinds of muscles are called **skeletal muscles** and you can move them when you want to.

Working alone

Your body has other kinds of muscle. **Smooth muscles** work automatically without you asking them to. They operate all over your body: for example, in your eyes, to focus and alter how much light gets in. The bladder has smooth muscles which remain relaxed until you want to go to the bathroom, when they contract to push the urine out. Your heart is a special muscle called cardiac muscle, which works by itself all day long to pump blood in and out.

Predators such as crocodiles and big cats have the strongest jaw muscles.

FACT 25

Shivering is caused by lots of muscles shaking at once to produce heat.

Bitesized facts

The muscles in your jaw help you talk, bite, and chew. They are extremely strong in humans, but even stronger in some animals. A crocodile's jaw snaps shut with a bite force that is nearly twenty times stronger than a person's. However, the muscles that open a crocodile's jaw are extremely weak; a croc's snout can be held closed with a rubber band!

YOUR DIGESTIVE SYSTEM WORKS UPSIDE DOWN

You don't have to be upright for food to work its way down through your body. Muscles in your digestive system push food along, whichever way up you are.

Keep on moving

Food starts as a solid item. When you chew, it is mixed with saliva (spit) and broken down into a more mushy lump. This is pushed down your throat and begins its journey down a tube to your stomach. The walls of the tube are lined with muscles, which tighten and relax in waves to move the food along its path. It only takes a few seconds, even if you are lying down or standing on your head!

> YOUR MOUTH WILL PRODUCE ENOUGH SALIVA IN A LIFETIME TO FILL TWO SWIMMING POOLS.

A long journey

Once the food reaches your stomach, it mixes with gastric juices that help to break it down. The stomach walls have their own set of muscles to mash things around and speed up the process. After a few hours food passes into the small intestine, then on into the large intestine. The good stuff is absorbed into the blood stream, and any extra water and waste products are disposed of when you next go to the toilet.

Different diets

A human's digestive system is designed to handle all types of food, from cereals to meat to fruit and vegetables. Other animals have adaptations to suit their diet. Carnivores such as lions have a simple system with strong stomach juices to break down meat. Herbivores such as horses, cows, and deer have extremely long intestines, often 20 times longer than their body. Plants need to stay in the body for more time because they are harder to digest.

THE SMALL INTESTINE IS ACTUALLY LONGER THAN THE LARGE INTESTINE, BUT IS NARROWER.

Fast food

A sea horse has no teeth or stomach. It sucks in tiny creatures and swallows them whole. It has a limited digestive system, so its food passes quickly through its body. It has to eat almost all the time to get enough nutrition to survive.

COCKROACH BRAINS CAN KILL DISEASES

Those nasty insects that scuttle across the floor could, in fact, contain life-saving molecules. Other creepy crawlies, such as locusts, have antibiotic qualities as well.

BACTERIA ARE MICROSCOPIC (TINY) LIVING THINGS MADE OF JUST A SINGLE CELL.

New cure needed

Scientists constantly search for new drugs to cure common diseases. They have recently found substances inside bug brains that are harmless to human cells, but which kill off the **bacteria** that cause infections such as MRSA and e-coli. This is especially good news, as many diseases have become resistant to the drugs once used to treat them, so we need new ways of wiping them out.

COCKROACH CURE
Take one pill a day for one week.

GRASSHOPPER TREATMENT
Warning: side effects include hopping and jumping

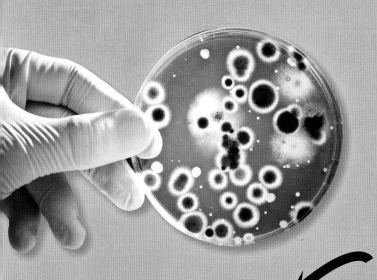

Beat the bacteria

Antibiotics have been found in soil and fungus. They can also be artificially created in the lab. They fight against bacteria to stop a person feeling ill. Bacteria can live and grow anywhere that isn't too clean: that's why hospitals must be spotless and germ-free. Bacteria are responsible for infections such as sore throats, earache, blood poisoning, and acne. Penicillin was the first antibiotic, discovered by Alexander Fleming in 1928.

Vaccinate a virus

Viruses are even smaller than bacteria, and cannot be treated with antibiotics. They cause illnesses such as flu, chickenpox, and measles. In 1796, Edward Jenner experimented with **vaccines** to fight against viruses. A tiny amount of the virus germ is injected into the body. The body naturally fights against it and becomes immune to it. If you are exposed to a larger amount of the virus, your body knows how to fight it and doesn't get sick.

FACT 28
Fleming discovered penicillin accidentally. It was growing on his lab equipment when he returned from a trip.

FACT 29
Vaccinations against seven major diseases (smallpox, diptheria, polio, measles, yellow fever, whooping cough, and tetanus) save nine million lives every year.

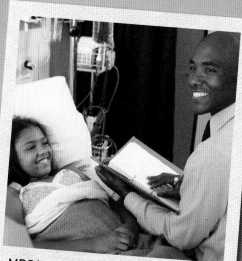

MRSA can spread easily in a hospital. Wash your hands!

FACT 30 CACTUS SPINES ARE REALLY LEAVES

The leaves of a plant are vital. They take in energy from the Sun so the plant can grow. The leaves of a cactus have turned into spines, and can be furry or extremely sharp.

Finding food

Animals and plants need food to grow. Animals have to move around to find something to eat, but plants do not. They put down roots to gather goodness from the soil (see page 40), and have leaves to take in carbon dioxide from the air and energy from the Sun. These three things combine in a process called **photosynthesis**, to make the food that the plant needs.

SPINES ARE A TYPE OF LEAF, BUT THORNS (LIKE THE ONES ON A ROSE STEM) ARE A TYPE OF BRANCH

Hello sunshine

Leaves contain a green chemical called chlorophyll to capture sunlight. The energy is used to create sugar so the plant can grow. Some of the energy can be stored, so the plant can still grow when there is less sunlight: during the winter or even at night.

All shapes and sizes

Leaves grow from a stem, and appear in a variety of shapes and patterns. Blades of grass, prickly holly leaves, pine needles, the fronds of a fern, and the distinctive three-part maple leaf show just some of the variety of shapes. Plants in poorly lit areas tend to grow larger leaves to gather more light. If the leaves become infected or die, the plant cannot produce food.

FACT 31

Originally, carrots were purple or white. Farmers bred them to obtain the orange variety we eat today.

Changing seasons

Deciduous plants lose their leaves before winter. There is not enough sunlight for photosynthesis to happen, so the leaves are not needed. The chlorophyll disappears, leaving the leaf's natural orange, red, or yellow to show through. Evergreen plants, such as holly, ivy, and pine trees, do not shed their leaves in cold weather.

FACT 32 TOMATO PLANTS ARE CARNIVOROUS

Plants need water, air, light, warmth, and nutrients. Many nutrients come from the soil, but some plants have other ways of getting the goodness they need.

More food, please

The process of photosynthesis (see page 38) involves more than just sunlight. Plants combine the energy they get from the Sun with carbon dioxide from the air, water from the ground, and nutrients. These nutrients are often found in the soil, but plants that grow in poor soil may catch insects as an extra food supply. The tiny hairs on a tomato plant stem trap bugs, and then the roots soak up the nutrients when the insects fall to the ground and decay.

Come on, flies, I'm hungry!

Meat-eaters

Insects can be caught in different ways. Some plants lure them in and then snap shut to prevent them flying out again. The pitcher plant has sugary nectar that smells sweet enough to eat. A hungry insect follows the scent into a cup-shaped leaf with deep, slippery sides that form a prison. The insect drowns in a pool at the bottom and becomes liquid plant food.

Frogs and rodents can drown in the biggest pitcher plants!

FARMERS ADD NUTRIENTS SUCH AS NITROGEN AND PHOSPHORUS TO THE SOIL IN THE FORM OF FERTILIZER.

Breathing out

When animals breathe, they take in oxygen from the air, and produce carbon dioxide gas. Plants do the opposite. They gather carbon dioxide and process it during photosynthesis. In return, they give off oxygen. Without plants, other living creatures would run out of the vital gas we need for life.

Living in the air

A small group of plants do not have roots growing in the soil. They grow on trees and rocks and get their moisture and nutrients through their leaves from the air, rain, and dust. They're called epiphytes.

FACT 33
ONE QUARTER OF OUR FOOD DEPENDS ON BEES

Our fuzzy, buzzy friends play a vital role in spreading plant pollen. As bee populations are getting smaller, that could mean big trouble for food crops.

EACH YEAR, BEES DO WORK THAT IS WORTH BILLIONS AND BILLIONS OF DOLLARS.

Plants need bees!

Plants use a powdery substance called **pollen** to reproduce, or make new baby plants. Bees gather it on their body as they feed on the nectar inside flowers. When they visit another flower, it rubs off and pollinates the plant, allowing fruit and seeds to grow. In this way, bees are essential to over 100 different foods, including apples, melons, broccoli, oranges, sunflowers, nuts, lettuce, onions, and beans. Without bees, farmers have to find expensive alternatives to pollinate their crops, or new plants won't grow.

Fruit bats spread pollen and seeds over great distances.

Useful pollinators

Bats, birds (especially hummingbirds) and flying insects transfer pollen. Plants use scents and bright flowers to attract pollinators. Grasses don't need pretty flowers, as their pollen is blown on the wind. Many plants also rely on creatures to spread their seeds far and wide. Birds and animals eat fruits and then leave the seeds in a different place in their droppings. Other seeds have tiny hooks that catch on fur to be carried far away.

Methods of transport

Seed dispersal can be quite spectacular or ingenious. Peapods ripen and burst, shooting their seeds into the air. Poppy seedpods sway in the wind, spreading their seeds like a saltshaker. Maple seeds act like tiny helicopters to spin through the air. Coconuts drop floating seedpods into water to be carried long distances. Oak trees drop shiny acorns that roll or are carried away by rodents. All plants benefit from spreading their seeds to avoid competing with them for sunlight and nutrients.

AN OAK TREE DOESN'T PRODUCE ACORNS UNTIL IT IS AT LEAST 20 YEARS OLD.

Little and large

Many seeds are tiny, but some grow to enormous sizes. Palm trees produce large seeds, such as the coconut. Often, they are waterproof and float for long distances on the ocean to find a new home. The coco de mer produces the largest seeds of all. They grow bigger than the cover of this book and the trees are a protected species. Avocados, mangos, and peaches grow some of the biggest seeds you will have seen.

43

FACT 34

GLASS CAN SURVIVE FOR A MILLION YEARS

Everything we grow, manufacture, and build uses energy and resources. Many of our actions create pollution and waste. If you throw away a glass bottle, it will stay in the trash forever.

Here to stay

Some things that we throw away rot into the ground. Food waste and paper are **biodegradable**: under the right conditions, they disintegrate naturally and quickly without causing harm to the environment. Many manmade products are harder to get rid of. Glass and plastic bottles don't break down, and may never actually disappear. It is much better to save them and reuse them. Not only does it solve the litter problem, it also uses much less energy than making new ones all the time.

RECYCLING ONE GLASS BOTTLE SAVES ENOUGH ENERGY TO POWER A COMPUTER FOR 25 MINUTES.

Using too much

Human activity takes its toll on the planet. Over 7 billion people live on Earth, and all of them need food and water, space to live, energy for lighting and heating, and other basics such as tools and transport. However, we are using the world's resources at an alarming rate, and causing many environmental problems along the way. **Ecologists** study the ways in which living things affect each other. They see how plants and animals work together to create an ecosystem, and look at how humans can affect it.

You can help

Around three quarters of human trash can be recycled, but it doesn't happen on its own. You need to do it! You can also help by using less water and electricity in your home, and less fuel when you travel. Everybody needs to learn the importance of saving the world's resources so our planet has a brighter future.

Ghastly garbage

Throwing things away is a bad idea. Everyday trash gets tipped into the ground as **landfill**, where it rots and gives off toxic waste that leaks into our water and escapes into the atmosphere. Leaving litter is dangerous to wildlife. Animals eat it and choke or are poisoned. Sea turtles mistake plastic bags for jellyfish and eat them. More than a million sea creatures die every year from ocean pollution.

Human activity means the Aral Sea, once used for fishing, no longer exists.

45

FACT 35

THE STATUE OF LIBERTY USED TO BE ORANGE

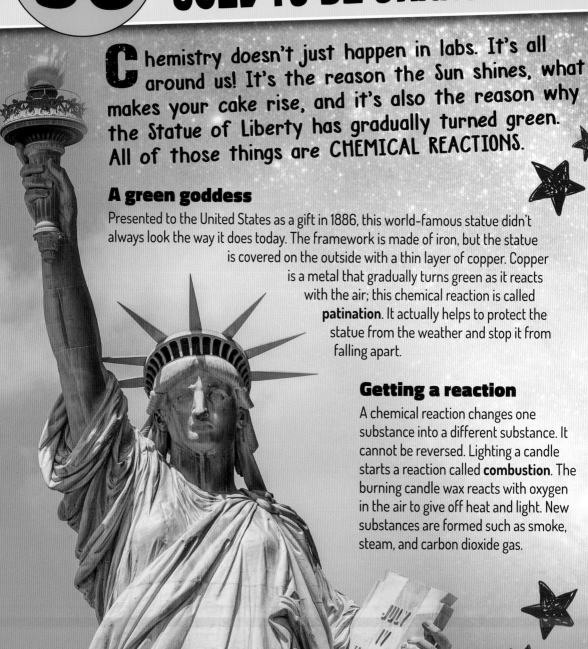

Chemistry doesn't just happen in labs. It's all around us! It's the reason the Sun shines, what makes your cake rise, and it's also the reason why the Statue of Liberty has gradually turned green. All of those things are CHEMICAL REACTIONS.

A green goddess

Presented to the United States as a gift in 1886, this world-famous statue didn't always look the way it does today. The framework is made of iron, but the statue is covered on the outside with a thin layer of copper. Copper is a metal that gradually turns green as it reacts with the air; this chemical reaction is called **patination**. It actually helps to protect the statue from the weather and stop it from falling apart.

Getting a reaction

A chemical reaction changes one substance into a different substance. It cannot be reversed. Lighting a candle starts a reaction called **combustion**. The burning candle wax reacts with oxygen in the air to give off heat and light. New substances are formed such as smoke, steam, and carbon dioxide gas.

Why is my bike rusty?

When iron and steel come into contact with water and oxygen, they **oxidize**, making a new substance called rust. Water and oxygen are both found in the atmosphere, and even more water is added to the situation if you leave your bike out in the rain! Rusting is an example of **corrosion**. Painting the metal helps to protect it from rusting by sealing it against the corrosive substances.

 FACT 36 A rusty bicycle weighs the same as the original bike, even though it looks different.

Everyday occurrence

It's not only scientists who do science. If you bake a cake, you are using a series of chemical changes to produce something yummy. Striking a match, washing your hair, and using bug repellent are all examples of chemistry taking place.

Body basics

Your body is a giant laboratory with lots of chemistry experiments going on all the time. When you eat, your body uses chemical reactions to turn the food into energy. When you breathe, you take in air and use the oxygen to fuel your body's cells. During the process, a waste gas called carbon dioxide is produced. Even a scab forming on a cut is an example of a chemical process.

FACT 37 Mars is called the Red Planet because its surface is covered in red iron oxide, or rust.

THE STUDY OF CHEMICAL REACTIONS IN LIVING THINGS IS CALLED BIOCHEMISTRY.

ANTARCTIC SNOW DOESN'T MAKE SNOWBALLS

Snow needs to be slightly wet to squish and stick into snowballs, but Antarctic snow is too dry and powdery. That's why penguins don't have snowball fights.*

* It's one of the reasons. Also, they can't pick up snow with their flippers!

What's the matter?

When scientists study "stuff", they call it **matter**. Matter is everything: air, the ocean, your hand, this book. It exists in different **states** depending on how it behaves. The three basic states that you will recognize are solid, liquid, and gas. Changes in state happen with a change in conditions: for example, when the temperature rises or falls. Water is a liquid but can become a solid (ice) when it is cooled, and a gas when it is heated.

Spot the difference

It can be easy to see different states: ice looks totally different from water. But how do we describe them? Solids keep their shape at room temperature: a table does not change shape by itself. Liquids can flow, and take the shape of their container. A pint of milk can be the shape of the bottle or carton, or a puddle on the counter. Gases are often invisible, but they float around to fill the space they are in.

Liquids turn into solids when they reach their freezing point.

Changing states

Water changes state quite easily. Other things need more extreme temperatures to change from one state to another. These temperatures are known as freezing point, melting point, and boiling point. Ice melts into water at 0°C (32°F). Lava is molten or melted rock, with a temperature between 700 and 1,200°C (1,292 to 2,192°F)!

Watery world

There is plenty of water on our planet. Most of it is in its liquid state, but salty: the oceans contain about 96.5 percent of all the Earth's water. A lot of it is frozen in icecaps and glaciers at the poles. It also exists as moisture in the ground. When this comes into contact with hot rocks, the water is heated enough to turn into steam. This can escape through the surface as geysers (giant spouts of boiling water and steam) and hot springs.

GALLIUM IS A METAL WITH SUCH A LOW MELTING POINT THAT IT GOES RUNNY IN YOUR HAND!

DIAMONDS CAN BURN!

In 1772 a French scientist named Antoine Lavoisier used a giant magnifying glass to set fire to a diamond inside a glass jar. This experiment helped him find out all sorts of things about the chemical world.

A single substance

Lavoisier's experiment helped scientists with their discoveries about **elements**. An element is a pure substance that cannot be broken down into any other ingredients. Diamonds are made of the element carbon. When Lavoisier's diamond burned, it reacted with another element: oxygen. Together, the two elements formed a new substance: carbon dioxide gas.

POOR LAVOISIER WAS EXECUTED IN 1794 DURING THE FRENCH REVOLUTION. A JUDGE DECLARED THAT FRANCE HAD "NO NEED FOR SCIENTISTS". SHOCKING!

Charcoal and graphite (the "lead" in a pencil) are also pure carbon!

Tough as diamonds

Diamonds form deep below the Earth's surface. They are crystals of pure carbon that has been squashed and heated over millions of years. They are carried closer to the surface by magma currents, and dug out of the ground in diamond mines. Diamonds are the hardest substance we know, but because they are made of carbon (which is flammable) they will burn under the right conditions.

CARBON BONDS EXTREMELY WELL WITH OTHER ELEMENTS AND IS FOUND IN NEARLY 10 MILLION COMPOUNDS, OR CHEMICAL SUBSTANCES.

Building blocks?

All elements are made of tiny specks called **atoms**. They are so small, they cannot even be seen under a microscope. They are the simplest building blocks of the stuff around us: what scientists call matter. An element is pure because it is made of just one kind of atom. Carbon, oxygen, gold, hydrogen...they are each made of a different type of atom, that's why they are all unique.

A brief history of science

People in ancient times didn't know about elements. They thought that everything in nature was made up of air, fire, water, and earth. Alchemists tried to find a miracle potion that would make them live forever, or a way to turn common metals into precious gold. By the sixteenth century, many had left this magical approach behind, and a more modern science was born.

FACT 40
YOU ARE MADE OF STARDUST

Everything in the universe is made of the same chemical elements: you, your bed, the Moon...EVERYTHING. It was all formed at the heart of a star, way back when the universe began. How mind-blowing is that?

FACT 41

Over half the human body is made up of water, or H_2O, containing hydrogen and oxygen.

Written in the stars

When the early universe expanded, particles quickly clumped together into atoms. The first, and simplest, were hydrogen atoms. These in turn joined to form helium, creating stars. Gradually, more and more elements were formed. Those elements are found today in your body: calcium in your bones, iron in your blood, and lots and lots of oxygen, carbon, and hydrogen.

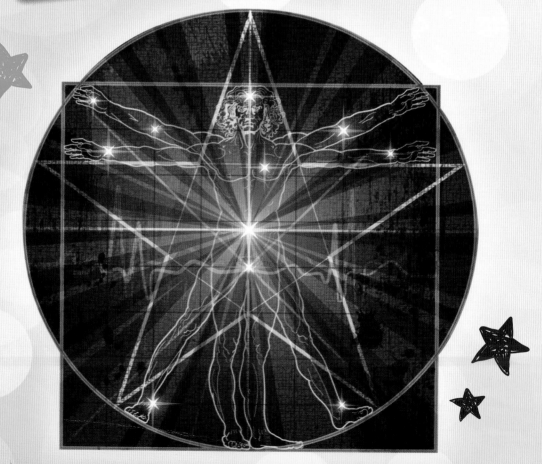

The number of electrons is different in every element.

So THAT'S what an atom looks like...

It's a small world

Atoms are tiny, but they are made up of even tinier ingredients: protons, neutrons, and electrons. Protons and neutrons sit together in the middle, called the nucleus. Electrons spin around this nucleus like planets around a Sun.

Light creates light

The nuclei of atoms join together to form new elements. This is called **fusion**. In space, gravity pulls together light elements and intense heat fuses them into heavier elements. So from the two lightest elements (hydrogen and helium) we get lithium, carbon, nitrogen...all the way up to iron.

FACT 42

Atoms are so small that if you lined up an atom for every person on Earth, they would only form a line about 1 m (3 ft) long.

Life story of a star

A star is a ball of elements, all fusing together and giving off light. A large star is hot enough to create some elements, but not all. When a star runs out of hydrogen it begins to collapse and get even hotter. This extra heat allows the creation of heavier elements. The dying star (called a **supernova**) pulses and eventually explodes, sending all of its elements out into space. Sometimes two dying stars may collide, producing all sorts of heavier elements.

53

FACT 43 TABLE SALT IS MADE OF TWO POISONS

Don't panic! It is still safe to sprinkle salt on your fries. Salt is a compound: a special chemical mix of different substances. When they bond together, the new substance can be completely different from the original ingredients.

Something new

Atoms are building blocks that can be joined together in different ways. Salt is made up of two types of atom: sodium and chlorine. Sodium is a silvery white metal and chlorine is a greenish gas, and both are extremely poisonous in some of their forms. However, they can be bonded together to form sodium chloride (NaCl), which is the white crystalline substance you use in cooking.

ALL ELEMENTS HAVE THEIR OWN CHEMICAL SYMBOL OF ONE OR TWO LETTERS.

SALT

FACT 44 Your body needs salt to work properly. It contains about 250g (9 oz) of the stuff.

Mmm, that lovely swimming pool smell!

You can usually smell the chlorine in the water, but it is perfectly safe.

Safe water

Chlorine acts really well as a disinfectant, to kill off germs. It can be added to water in tiny quantities to make it safe to swim in or drink. Most swimming pools and water companies prefer to use a powder or liquid that contains chlorine, instead of storing poisonous chlorine gas.

Crunching on crystals

Look carefully at table salt and you should see that it is made of tiny, regular cubes called **crystals**. They are formed when water evaporates, leaving the sodium and chlorine atoms which are bound together by electrical forces, or **bonds**.

FACT 45

Salt, sugar, ice, pencil lead, diamonds, and rubies are all crystals! (But they're not all edible, obviously.)

Sun, sea, and ...salt?

The metal sodium cannot be found in nature, although it occurs in large amounts in its other forms. It is easily found as NaCl in seawater. It also forms beautiful salt flats such as this one in Bolivia. When prehistoric lakes dried up, the salt was left behind, forming a white crust.

RAIN CAN DISSOLVE BUILDINGS

Pollution in the air contains many nasty substances. Some of these dissolve in the rain, and fall to Earth causing damage to buildings, forests, food crops, rivers, and wildlife.

Acid rain

Lots of human activity creates pollution. Chemicals escape into the air and mix with the gases in the atmosphere. They react to form sulfur dioxide and nitrogen oxides, which dissolve easily in water. This makes sulfuric acid and nitric acid. These fall to earth as **acid rain**, dissolving soft rocks such as sandstone and limestone. The acid rain also gets into our rivers, killing off plants, fish, and other creatures that live there.

SNOW, SLEET, AND FOG CAN ALSO BECOME ACIDIC AND CAUSE DAMAGE.

Spreading the damage

Polluting chemicals rise high into the sky and are blown by the wind. They travel vast distances, so many countries are affected, even if they try to reduce their own pollution levels. Once the acid rain gets into the water system, it flows through all our streams and rivers, reaching lakes and reservoirs.

Cars and other vehicles burn fossil fuels and create acid rain.

Rain damage

Acid rain affects more than just our statues and buildings. It gets into the soil and stops trees growing. It kills off their leaves and needles, and makes them much more vulnerable to diseases, pests, and cold weather. It reduces crops of foods such as carrots and broccoli, and changes the soil so that some plants just won't grow.

VOLCANIC ERUPTIONS CAN CAUSE ACID RAIN, BUT MOST DAMAGE IS DONE BY HUMAN ACTIVITY.

Fossil fuels

Power stations are the main cause of acid rain. They burn fossil fuels (such as coal and gas) to generate electricity for us to use in our homes, schools, and offices. This releases large amounts of sulfur dioxide and nitrogen oxides. We need to find cleaner ways of making electricity, and to cut down on how much electricity we use, to help reduce acid rain.

POPCORN POPS WHEN WATER TURNS TO STEAM

Of all the different types of corn, only one will go POP! Even then, it needs the right conditions. The most important thing is that it contains the correct amount of water.

How popcorn pops

A kernel of corn is made up of a hard outer shell, with a starchy substance and a small amount of water inside it. At a hot enough temperature the water becomes steam. This makes it expand, so it breaks open the hard shell. The inside turns fluffy, the steam escapes, and you hear the characteristic POP!

A CORN KERNEL GROWS UP TO FIFTY TIMES BIGGER WHEN IT POPS.

FACT 48

Fizzy candies react with your spit! The moisture dissolves the crystals and makes them fizz.

Getting bigger

Why does water expand when it turns to steam? Like so many things in chemistry, It all boils down (groan...) to molecules and matter. A molecule is a group of atoms bonded together. A water **molecule** contains two atoms of hydrogen (H) and one atom of oxygen (O), or H_2O. The molecules in a gas move more quickly than in a liquid, and they are more spread apart: they occupy more space.

Coffee beans contain over 800 chemicals mixed together.

Food for thought

All sorts of chemical processes take place in the kitchen. Baking powder releases bubbles of carbon dioxide gas, which makes cakes rise. Cooking meat breaks down the protein molecules, which makes it more tender. Boiling carbohydrates like pasta or rice makes the starch in them swell and soften. Toasting bread breaks down the chemicals and turns them into carbon, making it go brown. Who knew cooking was such a science!

In the mix

A simple food can be made up of many different chemicals. Food scientists can extract these chemicals and use them artificially to create different tastes. For example, the chemicals from citrus fruit skins can be added to food to make it taste like lemons. However, these chemicals don't dissolve in water, so they can't be used to make lemon drinks. Many chemists are employed by the food industry to figure out how these things work.

FACT
49

Fresh eggs sink but stale eggs float in a bowl of water, because they have more air inside.

59

FLOUR CAN EXPLODE

Don't be scared of baking, though. It won't happen in your kitchen! However, under the correct conditions, a cloud of fine powder can cause an explosion.

DUST EXPLOSIONS ARE OFTEN USED FOR SPECIAL EFFECTS ON FILM AND TV.

A big bang

Explosions are **chemical reactions** that need the right ingredients before they can happen. Tiny particles in a confined space can react with oxygen from the air and produce a big bang. It doesn't happen all the time; they also need something hot to ignite them. This may be a flame or a spark, but could also be a hot part of a machine, friction (two things rubbing together), or static electricity.

Pack it in!

The reason flour dust burns is that the particles are so tiny. They have a large surface area compared to their overall mass*. The surface of a substance is the part that burns, so more surface means more potential to catch fire. A tightly packed material has less surface area, so is less flammable.

*Mass is the amount of "stuff" in something. A bowling ball has more mass than a balloon the same size.

Death by dust

Flour isn't the only substance that is dangerous in dust form. Any fine powder will burn under the right conditions: spices, coal dust, powdered metal, and even sugar. In 2008, 14 people died in a sugar explosion in the US.

HIGHLY FLAMMABLE

Danger, danger!

Ready to explode

A pile of flour won't burn, even if you hold a flame to it. Nor will a bag of flour. The tiny particles of flour have to be dispersed in the air, as they are in a container such as a storage silo. It can be a huge danger in industry, where storing and transporting powder can create the exact conditions needed for it to explode.

This is why you're told not to throw flour around when you're cooking...

FACT 51

THE PERIODIC TABLE BEGAN AS A GAME OF CARDS

Scientists in the 1800s tried to arrange the elements in patterns according to their properties. In 1868 a Russian chemist playing Solitaire realized that cards with the elements written on them could be laid out in a similar way... and scientific history was made.

Looking for patterns

This Russian was Dmitri Mendeleev. He improved upon the work of chemists such as John Newlands, who had begun to arrange the elements starting with hydrogen (the lightest) as number 1. Mendeleev's card-game layout also took into account the elements' physical properties (what they look like, such as shiny solids) and chemical properties (for instance, how they react with other elements).

I'm taking a gamble on this theory...

Dmitri Ivanovitch Mendeleev
(1834-1907)

THE ROWS IN MENDELEEV'S TABLE ARE CALLED PERIODS: THAT IS, REPEATING SETS OF LINKED ELEMENTS. THAT'S WHY WE CALL IT THE PERIODIC TABLE.

Rising numbers

The elements in the table are laid out according to their **atomic number.** This is the number of protons in the nucleus. Hydrogen appears first as it has just one; oxygen is further along as it has eight; iron (the "heavy" element formed in stars) has 26. Each element also has an **atomic mass**: the number of protons plus neutrons it contains. These increase as you move further down the table, too.

Solitaire and the periodic table use rows and columns. Ask Granny to show you!

FACT 52

Most of the elements on the periodic table are metals.

Filling in the blanks

As Mendeleev arranged the elements, he realized that there were some gaps. Instead of rearranging them to fill the spaces, he made a great scientific leap. What if, he thought, we hadn't yet discovered all the elements? In fact, he even used their place in the table to predict what type of elements would fit in the holes. And he turned out to be right.

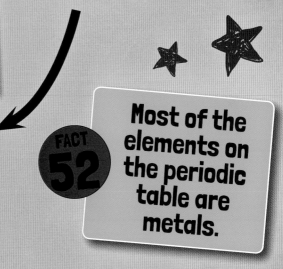

31
Ga
69.723

Are you sure?

Mendeleev was so convinced his theories were right that he questioned other scientific discoveries. He felt that there must be missing elements with predictable properties, and in 1875 a Frenchman, de Boisbaudran, discovered gallium, which seemed to fit one of the gaps. However, his measurements did not tally with Mendeleev's predictions. Mendeleev asked him to remeasure it, and the Frenchman found he had made a mistake!

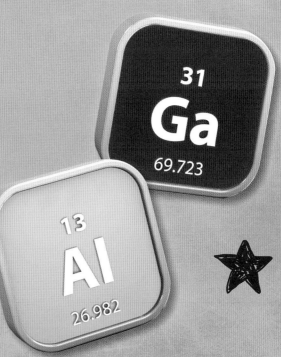

13
Al
26.982

FACT 53

THE WORLD IS RUNNING OUT OF HELIUM

Helium is the gas that is used to make balloons float. But there's bad news for birthdays, as it's in short supply! When helium is released into the atmosphere, it drifts off into space, never to return.

AT THE COLDEST TEMPERATURES, HELIUM BECOMES A LIQUID THAT CAN CLIMB UP THE WALLS OF CONTAINERS BY ITSELF!

Restricted resources

There are 118 elements in the periodic table, but not all of them are common, or easy to obtain. Helium is the second most abundant element in the universe, but is only produced on Earth by the breakdown of ancient rock, deep underground. The small amount of the gas that is trapped in the Earth's core must be carefully handled, as it is used for much more important things than party balloons.

Making it up

It sounds like nonsense, but not all of the 118 listed elements actually exist. That is: they can't be found naturally. Twenty of them (with atomic numbers 99 to 118) have only ever been made under laboratory conditions. Nine more were created artificially and helped fill the gaps in Mendeleev's table, but have since been found on Earth.

The name game

Many of the elements that were first discovered have descriptive names. Helium comes from the Greek *helios* which means Sun, as that is where it was first observed. Another gas, krypton, means hidden, because it is almost undetectable. Later elements are often named after the scientist who discovered them, or the place where the scientist lived.

Helium can be used in scuba tanks to allow divers to explore at greater depths.

THE TWENTY MAN-MADE ELEMENTS ARE CALLED SYNTHETIC ELEMENTS.

What else is helium used for?

Helium is extremely useful in medicine and scientific research. Liquid helium is so cold it can stop machinery from overheating. MRI scanners in hospitals use it, and so do superconducting magnets like the ones in the Large Hadron Collider at CERN in Switzerland. This is a giant underground tunnel where scientists recreate and study the conditions found at the beginning of the universe.

Endangered species

Scary newsflash: humans are using up the world's resources of precious elements. Several of these are known as Rare Earth Elements and are really hard to extract from the rocks where they are mined. But we are demanding them more and more, as they're vital ingredients in today's gadgets and technology, from headphones and hybrid cars to drugs and pacemakers.

WATER CAN MAKE THINGS EXPLODE

An element's place in the periodic table can give you a clue as to what it is like. Some are highly reactive, even with water. Potassium has to be stored in oil to keep it safe!

An explosive group

The elements in the first column (called group 1) of the periodic table are all known as **alkali metals**. Each of them reacts strongly with water and air; the lower down the group, the more reactive the metal is. Storing potassium in oil keeps it away from oxygen and water in the air. Further down the column we find rubidium, which explodes so violently in water that it can shatter its container!

FACT 55 Potassium is a metal but is soft enough to cut with a knife.

Judging a book by its cover

You CAN judge an element by what's on the outside. Its electrons are arranged in circles, and the outer circle makes a big difference to how much an element reacts. Some elements have a neat, full set of electrons and are happy to stay that way: they are the least reactive. Others have gaps to fill, or spare electrons to get rid of, so they share or swap electrons with other elements. These ones are more reactive.

by
M.T. Spaces

No reactions

At the opposite side of the table, in group 18, we find the **noble** gases. These have a full outer circle of electrons so are very unreactive. They include helium, neon, argon, and krypton, which can all be used to make decorative electric lights.

What shall I discover today?

Davy's discoveries

An extremely important English chemist named Humphry Davy discovered many of the group 1 and 2 metals. He was a big fan of electrolysis: passing electricity through liquids to separate them into different substances. He identified sodium, potassium, calcium, magnesium, boron, and barium using this method.

FACT **56**

Your body needs potassium to stay healthy. It is found in potatoes, spinach, mushrooms, and bananas.

Sir Humphry Davy
1778–1829

FACT 57

BANANAS ARE RADIOACTIVE

These tasty fruits contain high levels of potassium, which your body needs, so that's a good thing. However, potassium atoms are unstable and decay (break down), making them radioactive.

What makes something radioactive?

Every element in the periodic table has a set number of protons. Potassium always has 19, and that's what makes it different from oxygen, or silver, or neon. Usually, the number of protons matches the number of neutrons, but sometimes an element can be unbalanced. It has different **isotopes**, containing more neutrons than protons. Some isotopes are unstable, with too much energy. This is released, and the element is said to be **radioactive**.

OTHER RADIOACTIVE FOODS INCLUDE BRAZIL NUTS, CARROTS, AND POTATOES.

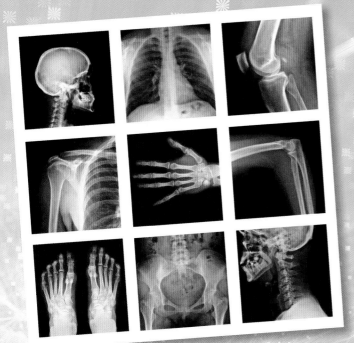

Radiation all around

Many radioactive elements are found in the natural world: in rocks, in water, and all around us in the stars and space. Scientists have learned how to make use of these elements for all sorts of helpful things. They are used in medicines, X-ray machines, smoke detectors, and to tell how old rocks and fossils are.

Danger! Danger!

High levels of radioactivity are dangerous to living creatures. The energy from the particles can pass through skin, and straight into the cells of the body. It damages the cells and causes radiation sickness. The body can't work properly anymore, and so people become ill, or even die. People who work with radioactive substances wear protective clothing and limit the time they spend exposed to radiation.

> This phone has me in peels of laughter.

Risky radiation

Bananas are safe to eat. They don't have high enough levels of radioactivity to do you any harm at all. You would have to eat millions and millions of bananas for the radioactivity to be dangerous. But a whole bunch of them just might contain enough radioactivity to register on a Geiger counter. That's a machine that counts how many radioactive particles are present. They show up on a screen, but also make a click. The faster the clicking, the more particles there are zooming around.

69

SALT CAN MAKE WATER SHRINK

If you slowly pour table salt into a full glass of water, the water level will go down! It's magic! Except of course it's not: it's science.

What's happening?

You would expect that adding salt would make the water rise and spill over the edge. Before that happens, though, scientific shenanigans take place. It's complicated, but the salt crystals have a charge that acts on the water molecules and pulls them closer together. That makes the water take up less space. As more salt is added, however, it begins to fill up the gaps between the water molecules, until eventually the space is taken up (known as saturation point) and the water overflows.

THE OCEANS ARE SLOWLY GETTING SALTIER AS RIVERS CARRY ROCK SALTS INTO THE SEA.

Mixing it up

Generally, saltwater and fresh water mix quite easily. Try it: if you pour tap water into a glass of salty water it will mix together and taste less salty than the original. This usually happens when rivers flow into the sea. However, under certain circumstances, water does not mix so well. When the Rio Negro, with almost black water, meets the Amazon River in Brazil, the two rivers run side by side without mixing!

Different temperatures, speed, and density keep the two rivers separate.

A salty solution

Saltwater and fresh water have some different properties. Saltwater has different boiling and melting points from fresh water. Adding salt lowers the melting temperature, which is why we sprinkle salt onto ice to melt it.

Don't be dense

Saltwater also has a greater density than fresh water. A bottle of saltwater has more mass (see page 61) than the same sized bottle of fresh water. The saltwater has more molecules, so it is denser. Objects float if they are less dense than their surrounding substance. That's (partly) how giant ocean liners work; their insides contain enough air to make them less dense than the water.

THE DEAD SEA IS SO SALTY IT IS VERY DENSE. PEOPLE CAN FLOAT WITHOUT TRYING!

FACT 59 — CAT PEE GLOWS IN THE DARK

Freaky, huh? All urine, particularly cat urine, contains the element phosphorus, which glows yellowish-green when oxygen is present. It is even easier to see with a black light or ultraviolet light.

MUCH OF THE PHOSPHORUS ON EARTH WAS BROUGHT HERE BY METEORITES.

Way to glow

Black lights are the ones used in displays (at museums and theme parks) to make things glow and look spooky. They will make teeth and white clothes glow in the dark. In a dark room, these lights will pinpoint any puddles your pet cat might have left. Confusingly, some other substances are called "phosphorescent" because they glow, although they don't contain phosphorus!

TOO MUCH PHOSPHORUS IN RIVERS AND LAKES CAN CAUSE A BUILD-UP OF ALGAE.

Strike a light

Phosphorus exists in two forms: red and white. It is used to make matches as it is very flammable (it catches fire easily). Old-fashioned "strike-anywhere" matches contain white phosphorus. They can be rubbed against a hard surface to cause friction, which heats the white phosphorus and makes it ignite. Safety matches are more common these days, as they won't accidentally catch fire in the box. Red phosphorus is mixed into the sandpaper on the matchbox, and the match only lights when it is struck against the sandpaper.

Cowboys lit "strike-anywhere" matches on the soles of their boots!

Playing with fire

Phosphorus was first discovered in 1669 by a German alchemist named Henning Brand. He collected urine (buckets and buckets of it, yuck!) so he could boil it and try to turn it into gold. Instead, he noticed that it glowed in the dark... and burst into flames! He named it from the words meaning "light-bearer" in Greek.

Spread it around

Phosphorus is extremely important. Our bodies need it for our bones, teeth, cells, and DNA. It combines with other chemicals to form phosphates, which are also vital for plant growth. Farmers use it in fertilizers. Today, most of it comes from rocks, but in the nineteenth century, it was collected in the form of guano (that's the dung of bats, seabirds, and seals). Guano is increasingly popular again these days, as an organic alternative to other fertilizers.

FACT 60

COLA DRINKS CAN BE USED TO CLEAN TOILETS

Cola rots your teeth if you drink too much of it. But can you put cola drinks to work? The same ingredients that cause tooth damage can be useful for cleaning bathroom grime!

Acid attack

Cola contains many ingredients, including three **acids** (carbonic, phosphoric, and citric). Acids can be weak or strong, with the strongest ones able to corrode (eat away at) all sorts of things. They can irritate or burn your skin, and damage your tooth enamel, so you should limit how many soft drinks you have. The acids in cola will break down the dirt in a toilet bowl, leaving it shiny and clean when you flush!

IN THE MALDIVES ISLANDS, COLA IS MADE FROM SEAWATER WITH THE SALT REMOVED!

74

Bees use acidic stings to defend themselves.

Hey, ladies, we're famous!

Acids all around

Scientists use the **pH scale** to measure acidity. A neutral solution (like pure water) has a pH of 7. An acid has a pH value below 7. The closer it is to zero, the stronger it is. There are acids everywhere, without you even knowing it: milk contains lactic acid, tea contains tannic acid, and oranges and lemons contain citric acid.

On the inside

Our bodies contain various acids to help us function. One of them is found in your stomach: hydrochloric acid. It kills off harmful bacteria and helps to digest your food. It is so strong that your stomach has to produce a sticky mucus lining to prevent the acid eating the stomach walls! Your body also produces lactic acid when you exercise, and that's what can make your muscles ache.

The other end of the scale

Acids can be neutralized by **bases** or **alkalis**, which have a pH value above 7. They often feel slimy and soapy to touch. Bleach and caustic soda are strong bases that can burn your skin and hurt your eyes and throat. Weaker bases are used in toothpaste, antacid remedies, laundry detergent, and hair conditioner. Ocean water is weakly alkaline; it has a pH of around 8.

AN ALKALI IS A BASE THAT CAN BE DISSOLVED IN WATER.

FACT 61

THERE IS GOLD IN YOUR COMPUTER

Gold is an element that has some very useful qualities. It is used to make parts for computers and phones, although there isn't enough to make it worth pulling your old PC to pieces!

Simply the best

Electronic devices such as phones and computers need tiny metal parts called connectors that **conduct** (carry) electricity. Copper is a good, cheap conductor, but it doesn't carry electricity as fast as is needed inside a computer. Silver is the best conductor, but it reacts with air and moisture creating a thin layer of tarnish on the outside, which stops it from working properly. Gold is the best choice for the computer industry. It is a great conductor of electricity, and it is highly unreactive, so it doesn't tarnish or fall apart as it gets older.

THE CHEMICAL SYMBOL FOR GOLD IS AU. IT COMES FROM THE LATIN NAME FOR GOLD, WHICH IS AURUM.

FACT 62

There is more gold in 1 ton of PCs than in 17 tons of gold ore.

Gold is heavier than the other dirt, so it sinks to the bottom.

Panning for gold

Gold can be found in rocks; this is called gold **ore**. The ore is dug out of the ground at gold mines, and mixed with other chemicals to separate the metal from the rocks. Gold also occurs naturally in small lumps called nuggets, often in the sand and gravel in riverbeds. Gold prospectors use large, shallow pans to swirl the sand around and separate tiny bits of gold. Scientists think that most of the gold was brought to Earth from space by meteorites.

FACT 63 The oceans contain gold worth trillions of dollars, but it is too diluted to be worth trying to extract it.

Mega metal

Most metallic elements are shiny solids that conduct heat and electricity. Metals are also **malleable**: they can be hammered into new shapes without breaking. Gold is the most malleable of all metals. It can be beaten into thin sheets called gold leaf. A single gram can be flattened into a sheet the size of a (very, very thin) bath towel! It becomes see-through and is used as a coating inside space visors, to protect the astronaut from the Sun's harmful rays.

Perfectly precious

Why is gold so special? It is rare, but it is also beautiful and useful. Its appearance, and its resistance to decay, led to its use on many precious artifacts. It was used to show power and wealth, and is still valued today as currency and for decorative items, as well as in the computer industry.

IF YOU CAN SMELL CABBAGE, BEWARE!

The world's smelliest substance is a gas called mercaptan. It stinks of rotting cabbage, leeks and garlic, or even dirty socks. But it can save your life!

Early warning

Natural gas is used in many buildings for cooking and heating. It is transported through pipelines and used for water heaters, ovens, and radiators. Natural gas is extremely flammable. A tiny little spark can ignite it and cause a huge explosion. It is hard to tell it is there, as it has no smell or taste. So gas companies add tiny amounts of super smelly mercaptan, which acts as a warning if the gas is leaking into the air around us.

MERCAPTAN IS SO SMELLY THAT YOUR NOSE CAN SENSE ONE PARTICLE OUT OF A BILLION AIR PARTICLES!

What a whiff

Mercaptan gas gives an unpleasant aroma to many things. It's what makes a person's breath smell, and the nasty gases they release from elsewhere! It is found in some nuts and cheeses, and is also present in our blood and brains. Dead, decaying animals give off mercaptan gas. Scavengers such as the turkey vulture pick up on the smell to guide them to their next meal, and they have been seen circling overhead if there is a gas leak!

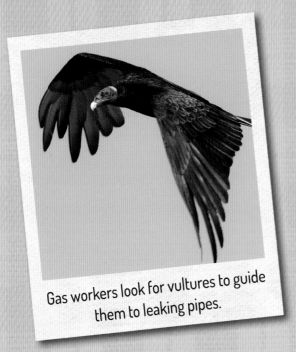

Gas workers look for vultures to guide them to leaking pipes.

SMELLY MERCAPTAN GASES FROM A LEAK IN A FRENCH CHEMICAL FACTORY SPREAD THE AWFUL STENCH FOR OVER 200 MILES!

Filling the space

All gases have certain things in common. Their particles are full of energy, and are free to flow in any direction they want. They spread out to fill whatever container they are kept in. You can see this in a balloon filled with air; no matter what shape you twist the balloon into, the air molecules still spread out through the whole balloon.

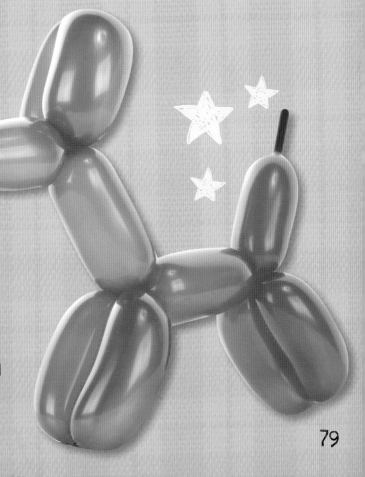

Changing state

Cooling natural gas changes it from a gas into a liquid. Its molecules slow down and take up less space. Natural gas can be stored at very low temperatures as LNG (liquefied natural gas) and transported in tankers instead of along pipelines.

DYNAMITE WAS FIRST CALLED "SAFETY POWDER"

Dynamite was invented in 1867 by the great scientist Alfred Nobel. It was intended to make it safer to blow up rocks for mining and building.

Boom-time

The nineteenth century was a time of exploration, invention, and development. People needed controlled explosions to blast rocks into pieces for building materials, or to make way for canals and train tracks. They often used gunpowder, but it was dangerous and not very strong. The other option was nitroglycerine, invented in 1847. The problem was, it was uncontrollably dangerous. Even a tiny jolt could make it explode, either while it was being transported or while the miners were putting it into the rocks.

ALFRED NOBEL HAD PATENTS FOR 355 OF HIS INVENTIONS AND IDEAS.

FACT 66

Dynamite has the same ingredient as cat litter.

FACT
67

Old dynamite leaks; the ingredients seep out and make it much more dangerous than new dynamite.

A safe solution

Alfred Nobel's family owned a nitroglycerine business, where his younger brother Emil was killed in a factory explosion. Alfred worked for years to find a way to make nitroglycerine safer to use. His solution was dynamite, which mixed nitroglycerine with diatomite (a kind of earth) that stopped it exploding by mistake. The dynamite was packaged in sticks, with a fuse to light them from a safe distance.

Making peace

Unfortunately for Alfred, his invention could also be used for violence and killing. When his brother Ludvig died in 1888, a newspaper mistakenly reported it as Alfred's death, and nicknamed him "The Merchant of Death." Alfred was devastated to read this, and swore to change his reputation. He decided to use his huge fortune to set up a prize fund for other great scientists. Nowadays, his name is remembered most in connection with the Nobel Peace Prize.

I just want a peaceful life...

Alfred Nobel
(1833–1896)

PLAY-DOH WAS INVENTED TO CLEAN WALLPAPER

Some of the best scientific discoveries happen by accident, while searching for a solution to a completely different problem. Play-Doh started life as a cleaning product!

PLAY-DOH IS MADE OF FLOUR, SALT, OIL, WATER, AND A WEAK ACID CALLED BORIC ACID.

Lateral thinking

In the 1930s, homeowners struggled to keep their walls clean. Their coal-burning fires left soot everywhere, and they used a white dough-like substance to clean it off. Unfortunately for the company that made this dough, the switch to cleaner fuels meant that their product was no longer needed. Cue one bright idea: add dye, give it a new name, and sell it to schools as clay for model-making!

A sticky situation

Scientists seem to struggle with sticky stuff. Some glue is too sticky, some is just not sticky enough. But add a creative mind, and you can find a use for either. Post-it notes were invented in 1968 when Doctor Spencer Silver was struggling to find an extra strong glue. Instead, he invented a less sticky glue that is ideal for attaching pieces of paper and peeling them off again.

By contrast, scientists in World War II were trying to find a clear plastic to make gun sights, but had problems because their product was too sticky. They were working with cyanoacrylate but it stuck to everything it touched! It took years for them to realize its potential as a "super glue," but now it is used for everything from mending mugs to fixing Formula One cars.

SUPERGLUE IS STRONG ENOUGH TO HOLD PARTS OF FORMULA ONE CARS TOGETHER, EVEN AT 200 MILES PER HOUR!

Sticky buns don't stick to Teflon!

A nonsticky situation

Teflon is the ultimate nonstick substance, used for baking sheets, cooking pans, and even hard-wearing clothes. Guess what? It was also discovered by accident, during an unrelated experiment!

FACT 69 CHOCOLATE IS POISONOUS FOR DOGS

Chocolate contains a chemical compound called theobromine. It is similar to caffeine, the chemical found in coffee and cola, and can be deadly if a dog eats it.

Out of reach

Chocolate and caffeine are **alkaloids**. They contain nitrogen molecules and are commonly found in nature. Like all poisons, the bigger the dose, the more dangerous it is. Dark chocolate contains more theobromine than milk chocolate, so is worse for a dog. A small dog will be badly affected by a small dose; even a chocolate chip cookie could cause problems. To play it safe, hide your treats from hungry pets!

Please? I would share my dog food with you.

A poison dart frog's bright skin is a warning that it is toxic.

Plants on prescription

Alkaloids are found in around one fifth of all plants. Poppies, tulips, lily of the valley, and daffodils contain them, as do the seeds of apples, cherries, and apricots. Each contains only a tiny amount, but it is best not to eat them! Throughout history, people have found how to use these poisons to their benefit. Some, like nicotine, are put in pesticides to kill insects. Morphine and codeine are ingredients in painkillers. Quinine was once the main treatment for the deadly disease malaria.

Poison arrows

Certain South American plants contain alkaloids that can be mixed to make curare. This is a deadly substance loaded onto arrow tips and blowgun darts. Once it enters the victim's blood it shuts down their system until they can no longer breathe. Some frogs secrete alkaloid toxins through their skin, giving them the nickname of poison dart frogs.

FOXGLOVE PLANTS CAN BE USED AS HEART MEDICINE, BUT WILL KILL YOU IN THE WRONG DOSE!

Fighting back

Snakes and spiders bite thousands of people every year, and some have a venom that can kill. Luckily, doctors can treat poisonous bites with an antivenom. Scientists collect the deadly venom and inject tiny doses of it into other animals, which build up an immunity in their blood. This blood can be gathered and used to treat people who have been bitten.

FACT 70

SOME CARS RUN ON HUMAN POOP

The world is running out of fossil fuels such as oil, coal, and gas. Scientists need to find other ways to supply energy for cars, homes, and factories.

A dirty business

Fossil fuels are a limited resource. Once we use them all up, there is no way of making any more. That's not the only problem: when we burn these fuels, they create pollution, and release greenhouse gases. These gases upset the balance of the Earth's atmosphere, which in the long term will have a damaging effect on life on this planet. But what alternatives are there?

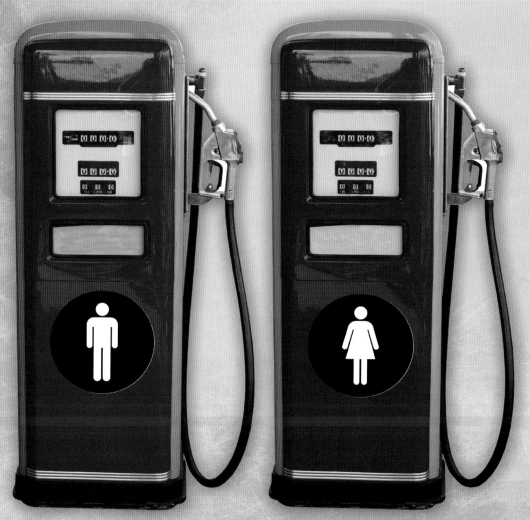

Biofuels

Cars and buses can be made to run on **biofuels**. Usually, these are made from plants, such as sugarcane, corn, and vegetable oil. They produce fewer harmful chemicals when they burn. However, they require large amounts of crops, which take up a lot of farming land and water for irrigation. Some people argue that it would be better to invest this effort and money into producing food, not fuel.

Cleaning up

One solution is to reuse waste products. Scientists have figured out how to convert human sewage and food waste into fuel. It is cheaper than converting crops into fuel, and recycles a product that nobody wants! Bacteria is added to the sewage to break it down and produce gas, which can be used for cooking and heating, as well as to power vehicles.

When you flush the toilet, the waste goes to a sewage treatment plant.

HENRY FORD'S EARLY CAR DESIGNS WERE INTENDED TO RUN ON PLANT-BASED FUEL.

Maybe I can help?

Waste wanted

It's not only human waste that has potential as fuel. Plant waste, such as corncobs and stalks, can be turned into ethanol but it is a tricky process. Scientists have found that pandas have just the right bacteria for breaking down tough plant waste. Further studies could help us solve our fuel problems... and help to save an endangered species, too.

Physics

FACT 71

LIGHT IS 18 MILLION TIMES FASTER THAN RAIN

Light travels through space at a constant speed. It is the fastest thing there is. Rain travels at varying speeds, but it's certainly a lot, lot slower than light!

Space travel

In the vacuum of space, where there are virtually no atoms to slow it down, light travels 299,700 km (186,000 miles) in a second. It takes about eight minutes for the Sun's light to reach us, here on Earth. **Astronomers** (scientists who study space) use the speed of light to measure vast distances in the universe. A light-year is the distance that light can travel in one year. Our galaxy, the Milky Way, is about 150,000 light-years across.

LIGHT CAN TRAVEL AROUND THE EARTH SEVEN TIMES IN ONE SECOND.

On the move

Light is a form of energy that travels in waves. It moves in a straight line, which is why you cannot see around a corner! It can pass through some things, such as air or water, but the particles in those things slow it down. It can also pass through transparent objects, such as glass. It cannot pass through some things, such as bricks or trees. These items are said to be **opaque**.

Playing with light

There are three main ways to control light. It can be blocked by objects, forming a shadow. It can also be bounced back, or **reflected** (see page 91) and bent, or **refracted** (see page 92).

TRANSLUCENT MATERIALS ALLOW SOME LIGHT TO PASS THROUGH, BUT NOT ENOUGH TO SEE THROUGH IT CLEARLY.

Hot and cold

Light energy often goes hand in hand with heat energy. A lightbulb gets hotter as it gives off light. A burning candle emits both light and heat energy together. Hot light is called **incandescence**. However, not all light sources give off heat. Cold light is called **luminescence**, and is found in nature. Fireflies and many deepsea creatures create their own cold light by mixing different chemicals in their body. This is the same kind of light as a party glowstick. When you snap the stick, you allow the chemicals to mix together and cause a reaction that gives off light energy.

FACT 72

THE HUBBLE TELESCOPE CANNOT LOOK AT THE SUN

The Hubble Space Telescope (HST) was the first telescope to view space from above the Earth's atmosphere. It can see galaxies that are trillions of miles away, but it cannot focus on the Sun without frying its delicate equipment.

High in the sky

The HST is not a telescope that you look through with your eye pressed up to it. It uses a digital camera to take photos, and beams them back to be studied in detail. Before the invention of the HST, telescopes were pointed into space from the Earth's surface. They have to look through the atmosphere, which changes and blocks some of the light. Hubble orbits above the atmosphere, so it can see more clearly.

THE HUBBLE TELESCOPE WAS LAUNCHED IN 1990 AND IS ABOUT THE SIZE OF A LARGE SCHOOL BUS.

I'm seeing stars!

Isaac Newton
(1642–1727)

Reflecting light

Light travels in straight lines (see page 89) and bounces off objects that get in its way. If the object is smooth and shiny, like a mirror or a smooth lake, the light reflects back to produce a clear image. If the object is irregular, like wind-blown water, the light is reflected in several directions and the image gets disrupted.

Banish the blur

The earliest telescopes used for looking at the stars produced blurry images. In the 1680s Isaac Newton invented a new kind of telescope with mirrors inside, which gave a much clearer view of the night skies. Called a reflecting telescope, it has a curved mirror which collects light from a distant object and reflects it so it becomes focused, or clearer to see. Another mirror reflects this focused image out of the telescope through an eyepiece.

A clearer view

Many telescopes are placed in a dome-shaped building called an observatory. They are often built on mountaintops, where the air is thinner and the view is clearer. There are 13 different telescopes on top of Mauna Kea, a dormant volcano in Hawaii. The island's position near the Equator, in the middle of the Pacific Ocean, where the skies are dark, dry, and cloud-free, makes it a prime spot for looking far into space.

THE MAUNA KEA OBSERVATORY IS HOME TO THREE OF THE WORLD'S LARGEST TELESCOPES.

A rainbow is a spectacular light show that happens when sunlight and water droplets occur together. You will only see it if you are standing with the Sun behind you.

Dividing light

Sunlight is known as white light, but is made up of different shades combined together. A rainbow forms when light hits a raindrop and is **refracted**, or bent. The light rays slow down as they pass from air into water, and travel at different speeds. They reflect off the inside of the raindrop, and bounce back out at different angles. This forms the curved rainbow, with red at the top and violet at the bottom.

Rainbows—not just for rainy days.

Make a rainbow

White light can be split into its spectrum of shades using a prism. A prism is a triangular glass block that refracts light as it passes through. The light is separated according to its wavelengths. Red has the longest wavelength and so is refracted the least. You may notice the rainbow effect happening in other situations: a fountain, waterfall, or the spray from a hose can perform the same feat. If you view a rainbow from the air, such as from a plane, it can form a full circle.

Beyond the visible

There are some rays which the human eye cannot see. Infrared and microwaves have longer wavelengths, and radio waves have the longest wavelength of them all. Microwaves can be used for cooking, but also for carrying signals for phones. Ultraviolet (UV) light has a shorter wavelength than the violet part of the spectrum. It can cause sunburn and make things glow. The shortest wavelengths are X-rays and gamma rays, used in medicine for detecting broken bones or cancer.

FACT 74

Sunlight can be reflected twice inside a raindrop, forming a double rainbow.

Hidden from view

Humans can't see UV light, but some creatures can. Scientists have found that bees can see UV markings on flowers that guide them straight to the nectar supplies. Reindeer rely on UV light for finding lichens to eat. Some birds use UV patterns to distinguish males from females. It's a whole world that is invisible to humans!

FACT 75

YOUR EYES SEE UPSIDE DOWN

Light bounces off objects and into your eyes, where the image is passed to your brain to make sense of the world. But the image formed in your eye is flipped on its head!

> Now, how do I eat it?

THE LENS IN YOUR EYE CHANGES SHAPES TO FOCUS SO THAT YOU DON'T SEE BLURRED IMAGES.

Seeing the light

Light enters your eye through a section at the front, like a window, called the cornea. It passes through a curved lens which bends the light rays to focus them, and creates an upside-down image on the surface at the back of the eye. This surface is called the retina, and its function is to turn light into signals that your brain can understand. The brain very cleverly flips the upside-down messages so that you see the world the right way up.

Darkness and light

The retina has different types of cell to perform different jobs. It contains around 7 million cones, which are sensitive to red, green, or blue light. They work together to allow you to see millions of different shades. The retina also has rods, which see in black and white. They are sensitive to light and dark and allow you to see shapes and movement, even in very low light.

All in your mind

A strawberry is red, round, and you can feel its mass when you hold it, right? Well, kind of. It certainly has a definite mass, and shape, but its "redness" is something you see, rather than a physical quality. Light hits an object and either bounces off or is absorbed, depending on its wavelength. A strawberry absorbs all the light except the wavelengths that look red when they hit the cones in your retina. If you were a dog or a fish, you wouldn't see it as red at all.

CATS AND DOGS CAN'T SEE THE DIFFERENCE BETWEEN RED AND GREEN.

Playing tricks

Sometimes your brain can be tricked into seeing things that aren't real. Your eye gathers information that your brain tries to interpret and turn into some kind of sense. Optical illusions play with your vision and your brain to make you see things that don't match reality.

Too much visual information tricks the brain into thinking shapes are moving.

THE LOUDEST SOUND EVER WAS A VOLCANO

When Mount Krakatoa erupted in 1883 the sound was heard 4,800 km (3,000 miles) away in Mauritius. It was the loudest sound in recorded history.

What a noise

A volcano erupts when gas bubbles force magma (molten rock) high into the air. It creates sound waves that travel far around the Earth. All sounds are made when objects move or vibrate, making the air around them vibrate. The sounds travel as waves of energy that hit your eardrum. Your brain translates the vibrations in your eardrum into recognizable noises, whether it's a dog barking, a bell ringing, or a volcano exploding.

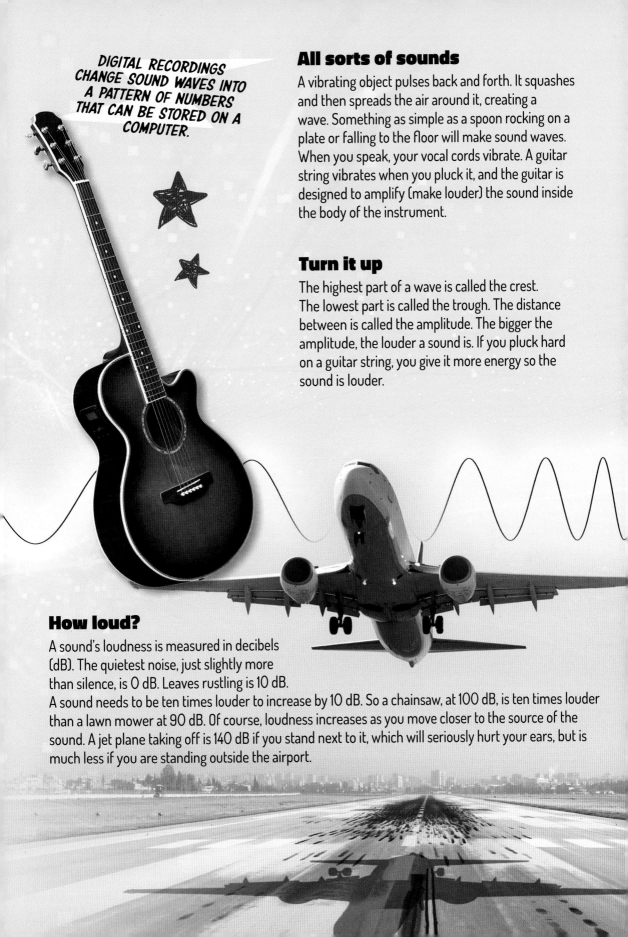

DIGITAL RECORDINGS CHANGE SOUND WAVES INTO A PATTERN OF NUMBERS THAT CAN BE STORED ON A COMPUTER.

All sorts of sounds

A vibrating object pulses back and forth. It squashes and then spreads the air around it, creating a wave. Something as simple as a spoon rocking on a plate or falling to the floor will make sound waves. When you speak, your vocal cords vibrate. A guitar string vibrates when you pluck it, and the guitar is designed to amplify (make louder) the sound inside the body of the instrument.

Turn it up

The highest part of a wave is called the crest. The lowest part is called the trough. The distance between is called the amplitude. The bigger the amplitude, the louder a sound is. If you pluck hard on a guitar string, you give it more energy so the sound is louder.

How loud?

A sound's loudness is measured in decibels (dB). The quietest noise, just slightly more than silence, is 0 dB. Leaves rustling is 10 dB. A sound needs to be ten times louder to increase by 10 dB. So a chainsaw, at 100 dB, is ten times louder than a lawn mower at 90 dB. Of course, loudness increases as you move closer to the source of the sound. A jet plane taking off is 140 dB if you stand next to it, which will seriously hurt your ears, but is much less if you are standing outside the airport.

DOGS CAN HEAR THINGS YOU CAN'T

A dog's ears collect more sounds than yours, and from farther away. But they also hear noises that are outside the range of human hearing.

High-pitched hearing

Some sounds are high; others are low. That's because they have different pitches, or frequencies. Frequency measures the number of waves per second in a sound wave, and it is measured in hertz (Hz). A high-pitched noise has more waves per second; the waves are squeezed closer together. Humans can only hear higher-pitched noises between around 20Hz and 20,000Hz. Dogs can hear much higher pitched noises: as much as 60,000Hz.

I hear breakfast being served...

LOW-PITCHED NOISES, SUCH AS THUNDER, HAVE A LONG WAVELENGTH.

Pitch perfect

A piano can make notes of varying pitch. The keys on the left make low notes, and the pitch increases as you move to the right. The strings attached to the keys are different lengths and thicknesses.

FACT 78

Sound travels more slowly than light That's why you see lightning before you hear thunder.

Whale song can travel through water for thousands of miles.

Moving sound

The energy in a sound wave passes easily between air molecules. Sound has to have a medium to travel through, such as air, water, glass, or metal. It cannot travel through a vacuum where there are no particles to carry it.

Animal song

Sounds that are too high-pitched for people to hear are called ultrasound. They can be used in medicine, to look inside the body and check blood flow. Many creatures have ultrasonic hearing, not only dogs. Bats and dolphins can hear over 100,000 Hz and use echolocation to find their way around and capture prey. They send out high-pitched sounds and listen to the echoes that bounce back. Low-frequency sounds travel long distances through water. Some whales "sing" as low as 30 Hz to communicate over thousands of miles.

Different notes

A musical instrument's pitch depends on the size of the moving part, or how tightly it is stretched. A small drum makes a higher note than a big drum. A short string makes a higher note than a long string. Many musical instruments make a range of sounds. A guitar's strings are different thicknesses, and can be tightened or loosened, to produce different notes.

FACT
79

Elephants can detect low sounds through their feet: as low as 5Hz.

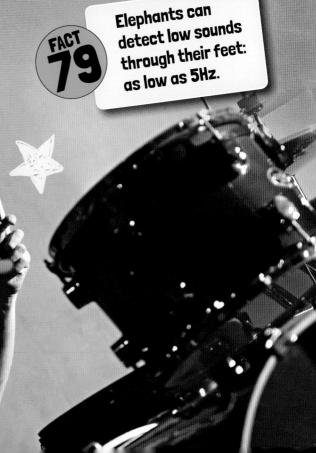

FACT 80

MARSHMALLOWS MELT AT MACH 1.6

Sound waves travel VERY quickly. Supersonic things move faster than the speed of sound, also known as Mach 1. That's fast enough to heat things up, making a marshmallow turn to goo.

What is the speed of sound?

The speed of sound is not a fixed number. Sound waves travel through air at around 340 m/s (760 miles per hour) at sea level. Sound travels four times faster through water than it does through air, and around 13 times faster through steel. However, high in the atmosphere, where it is colder, the speed of sound decreases. Mach numbers compare the speed of an aircraft to the speed of sound where the plane is flying. So, Mach 2 is twice the speed of sound in air at a particular height.

TWO ITALIAN SCIENTISTS WERE THE FIRST TO CALCULATE THE SPEED OF SOUND IN THE 1660S.

Moving sounds

Sounds change as they move. If you stand still and watch an emergency vehicle zoom past with its siren blaring, the noise will be higher pitched as it approaches, and lower pitched as it drives away. This is known as the **Doppler effect**. The sound waves are emitted at the same frequency, but because the vehicle is getting closer, they take less time to reach you, and arrive at a higher frequency. It makes the siren sound different.

A train's blaring horn changes sound as it goes past.

THE DOPPLER EFFECT HAPPENS WITH SOUND, LIGHT, AND WATER WAVES.

Supersonic

If the vehicle is moving faster than the sound waves can move, we hear a different effect. In this case, the sound waves bunch together and create a high pressure zone. This leaves an area of low pressure right behind it, and makes a really loud noise called a **sonic boom**.

Melting moments

Let's not forget the gooey marshmallows. An object zooming through the air doesn't have a smooth passage. It is constantly bombarded by the air particles, which slow it down and produce heat. This is known as friction, or air resistance, and would (theoretically!) heat up the marshmallow enough to melt it, if it was moving fast enough. Find out more about friction and resistance on page 120.

FACT 81

A RAMP IS A MACHINE

If you want to push an object to a higher point, you'll need a ramp. A ramp is a type of simple machine and it can be combined with other machines to make compound machines.

Scientific work

Physicists examine forces and the effect they have on objects. A force is a push or a pull, and can happen at a distance or by making contact. Machines apply a force to an object; they do **work**. A ramp is a simple machine, and so are levers, wedges, pulleys, screws, and the wheel and axle.

FACT 82

Mountain animals look for natural ramps to climb upward more easily.

A PLAYGROUND SLIDE IS ALSO AN INCLINED PLANE.

Moving up

A ramp (properly called an inclined plane) is a flat surface with one end higher than the other. It allows an object to be moved higher, using less energy than lifting it straight up.

More machines

If you put two inclined planes back to back, you get another simple machine: a wedge. It is used to push objects apart. A knife, a chisel, and even your teeth are all wedges. A screw is a special kind of inclined plane. It is wrapped around a central pole and helps to lift things or hold them together. A lever is a really simple machine that is used all the time. It consists of a straight bar resting on a fulcrum (turning point) to multiply the force used.

Combined power

A bicycle is a fine example of a complex machine that uses many simple machines together. It has wheels and axles, pulleys (the chain on the gears), wedges (the gear teeth) and lots of levers and screws. Luckily, operating this complex machine is simpler than describing it!

The Egyptians used machines such as ramps for building the pyramids.

FACT **83**

The pointed nose of a plane is a wedge, used for cutting through the air.

Move the levers around the fulcrum, and...snip!

Snip, snip!

Scissors are also a compound machine. The blades are a pair of wedges, attached to levers (the handles) which move around a fulcrum so they open and close.

FACT 84

A BATTERY AND BUNGEE JUMP BOTH STORE ENERGY

Energy is all around us, in all sorts of forms. It is simply the ability to do work. It can be stored up, ready to use when it is needed. This is called potential energy.

On your marks...

Energy can be stored electrically in a battery, to put in your phone or remote control for when you want to use them. Objects can also have potential energy because of their position. If they are high up, they have the potential to be moved by gravity. A book resting on the edge of a table, a ball held in your hand, or a bungee jumper about to leap off the edge all have potential energy.

FACT 85

Objects that spring or stretch, such as a trampoline or a rubber band, have elastic potential energy.

More energy

An object gains more potential energy as it moves higher. A heavy object has more potential energy than a light one.

THE ENERGY IN MOVING OBJECTS IS CALLED KINETIC ENERGY.

Get set...

An object can have potential energy if it is altered from its usual position. A spring at rest has no energy, but if you exert a force on it to squash it or stretch it, you transfer energy, which is stored until the spring is released again. The same happens when an archer draws back the string of a bow.

Go!

When an object starts moving, its potential energy is converted to kinetic energy. A sprinter in the blocks has potential energy until the gun goes and he or she starts running. If you climb a mountain, your muscles pull against gravity to move your body upward. You draw on your supplies of chemical energy from your food. As you get higher, you gain potential energy. At the top, you can turn this stored energy back into kinetic energy by abseiling down.

No pain, no gain

According to the laws of physics, energy can be converted from one form to another, but cannot be created or destroyed. The energy you use to climb the stairs is converted into potential energy by being higher up than you started.

FACT 86

Food contains chemical energy for living things to move, grow, and breed. It is often measured in joules or calories.

FACT 87

A KETTLE BOILS FASTER AT THE TOP OF A MOUNTAIN

The higher you climb, the less air there is around you. The lower air pressure allows liquid to turn into gas more easily, so the boiling point of water is lowered. A kettle will boil more quickly.

THE REDUCTION IN AIR PRESSURE ALSO MAKES IT HARDER TO BREATHE AT HIGH ALTITUDES.

Climbing high

The gases in the air are constantly pressing down on us. If we are low down, at sea level, the whole of the atmosphere is on top of us, creating higher air pressure. As we climb higher, there is less air above us, and the pressure is reduced. It means that the water molecules inside a kettle need less heat energy to turn from liquid to gas and reach boiling point (see page 107).

Under pressure

Pressure is the amount of force on a given area. A person wearing high heels is pressing with all their weight on a tiny space. Wearing snowshoes lowers the pressure, as a person's weight is spread across a much larger area. Pressure can be caused by many things. Water presses down, so there is higher pressure at the bottom of the ocean than on its surface. Deep-diving animals, such as sperm whales, have special lungs that can cope with being crushed.

Spreading your weight stops you sinking in the snow!

SCIENTISTS USE THE KELVIN SCALE TO MEASURE TEMPERATURE, RATHER THAN CELSIUS OR FAHRENHEIT.

A tight squeeze

How exactly does pressure affect temperature? Temperature is a measure of kinetic energy: how much the atoms are moving around. The atoms in cheese on a pizza have been given more energy by heating them. They are moving more freely, so the cheese melts and becomes runny. By lowering the air pressure, the atoms are less pressed together, so a smaller amount of heat is needed to free them from each other. It's like opening a jar of peanut butter: a loose lid requires less energy to take off than one that has been firmly screwed on.

Taking your temperature

Temperature can be measured with a thermometer. In many thermometers, a liquid is trapped in a glass tube. As the temperature increases, the liquid atoms move more and take up more space, so the reading on the thermometer goes up.

FACT 88

SNOW KEEPS YOU WARM

Snow is cold to touch, but if it is used to build a shelter against the cold air, it can stop the temperature from dropping. An igloo is much warmer inside than a tent.

In the air

Snow is made up of ice crystals that are packed together with a lot of air in between. Air is a poor conductor (carrier) of heat, and if it is trapped in one place, it prevents heat escaping. Heat travels from hot things to cold things, and moves through some substances better than others. Metals transfer heat quickly, so are good **conductors**. Gases (such as air), rubber, plastic, and wood, do not allow heat energy through so easily. They are good **insulators**.

ANIMALS' FUR TRAPS AIR NEXT TO THEIR BODY TO KEEP THEM AT THE RIGHT TEMPERATURE.

Moving around

Heat can move around in three ways: conduction, convection, and radiation. **Conduction** happens when two things touch. If you hold an ice pop in your hand, the heat moves through the particles. Energy transfers from the fast-moving particles to the slower-moving ones, so your hand cools down and the ice pop heats up and melts. The bottom of a lava lamp contains a heater, which conducts heat energy to the glass and the wax inside.

Convection currents

Heat can travel through a liquid or a gas by **convection**. The hot, melted wax in a lava lamp becomes less dense and so it rises. It shares its heat as it does so, cooling and sinking back down again. At the bottom, it receives more heat, and rises. This also takes place in a pan of soup, a hot air balloon, and in the atmosphere, creating weather.

THE STUDY OF HEAT AND ENERGY IN PHYSICS IS CALLED THERMODYNAMICS.

Radiating rays

Conduction and convection need particles to transfer heat. **Radiation** carries heat on waves of light, usually infrared rays (see page 93). It can work through the vacuum of space, where there are no particles. The Sun's warmth radiates through space to reach us here on Earth. Heat also radiates out from a campfire. A house radiator does not really radiate heat; it transfers it through the air by convection.

Radiated heat from the Sun heats up the Earth.

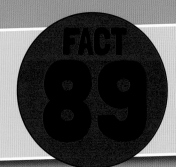

A BIRD ON A WIRE WON'T GET A SHOCK

Electricity wires are dangerous to people, but birds are quite safe... just so long they don't touch anything else! That's because the birds are not giving the electricity a route to the ground.

Do not touch!

Electricity is the movement of electrons. These tiny particles will move from an area of 'high electric potential' (where lots of electrons are packed) to an area of lower electric potential, where there is more room for them. The Earth itself is so huge that it has a very low electric potential. If you touch a wire while also touching the ground, the electricity will flow through your body to reach the area with lowest electric potential.

Flowing electrons

A battery has a positive end, which has a high electrical potential, and a negative end, with lower electrical potential. When a battery is in use, it creates a circuit. The electrical charge moving through a circuit is called **current**. Current is measured in amperes (shortened to amps, or A) which tell you how fast it flows. A bulb may have 1A of current, while a toaster uses about 9A.

Breaking the loop

Electricity makes things work at the flick of a switch. How does that happen? No current flows when the switch is off, because the circuit is broken. In the on position, the switch completes the loop, and your lamp, or kettle, or games console will work. A toy racing car has a metal contact which fits into a slot on the race track. When it touches the sides, electricity can flow.

I feel famous!

Power struggle

A battery supplies stored electricity to many toys and gadgets. The current flows from it in a single direction in a constant stream. It is called **direct current**, or DC. Household items that work from the mains use **alternating current**, or AC. The famous scientist and inventor Thomas Edison was insistent that DC current was the way forward, but his rival Nikola Tesla (1856–1943) proved otherwise.

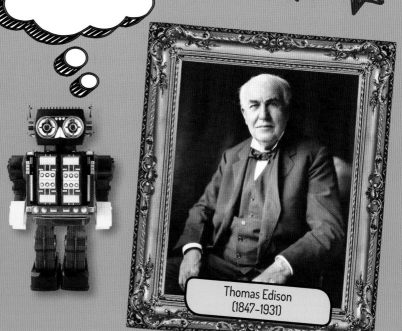

Thomas Edison
(1847–1931)

111

FACT 90 ELECTRICITY ZAPS BACK AND FORTH

If direct current (DC) flows in one direction, then alternating current (AC) constantly changes direction.

Back and forth

Mains electricity in your home is AC, not DC. When you plug in your TV, it connects to the electricity supply to give it power. The electrons in this circuit don't flow from point A to point B. Instead, they change direction 50 or 60 times per second, transferring electric current as they move. This cycle of changing directions is described as the frequency, and is measured in Hertz (just like sound waves; see page 98).

SOLAR CELLS CAN ONLY PRODUCE DC CURRENT. IT HAS TO BE CONVERTED INTO AC CURRENT TO BE USED IN THE HOME.

I'm certainly getting a shock!

Electricity flows like water, but don't mix the two of them!

ELECTRICITY IS GENERATED AT 25,000V, BUT SENT ALONG CABLES AT VOLTAGES UP TO 16 TIMES HIGHER.

Many measurements

Different properties of electricity are measured in different units. Hertz is the unit of frequency: how often it changes direction. Amps is the unit of current: how fast it is flowing. You will also hear volts and ohms. Imagine electricity is like water gushing out of a hose. As well as measuring how fast it flows you could also measure how much pressure is pushing it along; electrical pressure is measured in volts (V). A narrower hose will affect the flow, creating resistance, which is measured in ohms.

Making changes

Voltage, current, and resistance are linked. Altering one of them will affect the others. Imagine you turn up the pressure on your hose, or make the hose wider. More water will come out. Similarly, increasing the voltage or reducing the resistance will make more current flow.

Danger! High voltage!

Power plants send electricity over great distances. When electricity travels along cables, some energy is lost. If the current is reduced, so is the amount of lost energy. To reduce the current, the voltage is increased. High-voltage electricity travels extremely fast, but is very dangerous. Before it is delivered to our homes, it passes through a special transformer to reduce the voltage and make it safer (although it can still give you a nasty shock).

FACT 91 LIGHTNING STRIKES 100 TIMES EVERY SECOND

Lightning is a bright flash of electricity produced in a storm. It is very common: there are around 2,000 storms around the world at any time, most of them in the clouds.

Shocking!

Not all electricity flows in a current. Some is static electricity, which is electric charge that builds up in one place. It produces lightning, but on a smaller scale: it can cause the shock you feel when you wear certain shoes and then touch someone, or grab a metal door handle. It is caused by an imbalance between positive and negative electric charges.

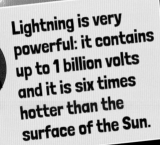

FACT 92

Lightning is very powerful: it contains up to 1 billion volts and it is six times hotter than the surface of the Sun.

Lightning strike

Frozen raindrops move around and bump into each other inside a storm cloud. The crashing around creates an electric charge, which is attracted to charges on the ground. Lightning zaps between the cloud and the ground to connect them. It is often called forked lightning because of the pattern it makes. Thunder occurs when the heat from lightning makes the air expand really quickly, causing vibrations.

In the air

Sometimes lightning stays within the clouds, as different charges at the highest points and lowest points are attracted to each other. Lightning in the air is often called sheet lightning. There are up to ten times as many flashes in the air as there are between clouds and the ground. Planes are often hit by lightning, but are protected so that the passengers do not get hurt.

AROUND 2,000 PEOPLE A YEAR ARE KILLED BY LIGHTNING STRIKES.

Getting to ground

Lightning tends to strike the highest thing in the area: a tree, an antenna, or a tall building. It can set them on fire and cause immense damage. In 1749, Benjamin Franklin, an inventor and politician, invented the lightning rod to protect buildings that may be struck. A tall metal pole on the roof is connected to a metal cable that leads to the ground. The metal conducts the electricity easily and quickly away from the building and into the earth.

The Empire State Building has a lightning rod as it is hit many times each year.

THE EARTH HAS TWO NORTH POLES

The Geographic North Pole is at the very top of the Earth, and is the point the Earth rotates around. The Magnetic North Pole can be nearby, but moves around all the time.

Mega magnet

The Earth has a central core of molten iron that swirls and creates electric currents. This produces magnetic fields, and turns the Earth into a giant magnet. Like all magnets, our planet has two opposite poles: north and south. The needle of a compass is attracted to the Earth's magnetic north, not to its true geographic north. Changes under the Earth's crust (top layer) make the magnetic north move on a daily basis.

AT THE NORTH POLE, THE SUN RISES IN MARCH AND SETS IN SEPTEMBER.

An electromagnet can be switched on and off to move metals around.

On and off

Magnets come in different sizes, shapes, and forms. A bar magnet is a simple example. One end is north, the other end is south. It is surrounded by an invisible magnetic field which attracts some metallic objects (those containing iron, steel, nickel, or cobalt). Small items can be made temporarily magnetic by rubbing them along an existing magnet. An electromagnet is made by passing an electric current around an iron core. If it is switched off, the iron stops being magnetic.

Opposites attract

If you hold two magnets together, they will act in different ways. If opposite ends (N and S) are together, they will be attracted and stick to each other. If like ends (N and N or S and S) are together, they will repel. You will feel them trying to push each other away. A maglev train uses this principle to make it hover above the tracks without touching them.

Magnetic marvel

The Sun belches out gases from its surface which make their way toward Earth. The magnetic field channels them to the poles where they bounce off oxygen and nitrogen atoms in the atmosphere, causing incredible light shows called the **auroras**.

A MAGNET STUCK TO YOUR REFRIGERATOR HAS MORE MAGNETIC FORCE THAN THE EARTH.

A BALL THROWN IN SPACE WILL NEVER STOP

If you throw a ball, it will keep going forever unless some sort of force acts upon it. On Earth, these forces include gravity and air resistance. Neither of those would really affect a ball thrown in space.

Down to Earth

All objects have their own gravity, pulling other things toward them. Generally it isn't strong enough to notice, but large objects (really large, like planets) have a gravitational pull that can affect other things. The Earth's gravity is strong enough to stop you floating off into space. If you throw a ball in the air, gravity brings it back down again. There are sections of space with nothing big enough to cause gravity.

THE MOON'S GRAVITY PULLS ON EARTH'S OCEANS, CAUSING THE TIDES.

It's the law

Gravity is a force, and acts on other objects to change them (see page 102). Scientists have three basic laws to describe motion and forces (thanks to Isaac Newton, who helped improve telescopes on page 91). It is the first of these laws that describes what happens with the ball in space. Namely, that any object in motion will continue to move in the same direction and speed unless forces act on it.

Large masses take larger forces to make them move.

A FORCE CAN MAKE AN OBJECT SPEED UP, SLOW DOWN, OR CHANGE DIRECTION.

Newton's second law...

...concerns forces, mass, and acceleration. Put simply, the more mass an object has, the more force it takes to make it move faster. It's obvious, really: it is harder to push a real car than a toy one. And if you exert more force, the car goes faster.

Number three

This law sounds complicated, but it really isn't. It states that for every action, there is an equal and opposite reaction. It simply means that when object A pushes on object B, object A gets pushed back in the opposite direction, equally hard. When you push back with your foot on the floor, it makes your skateboard move forward. When you sit on a chair, the chair (because of the materials and design) pushes back with an equal force, so it doesn't collapse and send you crashing to the ground.

FACT 95

SKIERS DON'T SKI ON SNOW

A ski presses down on compacted snow and melts a thin layer into water. The water reduces friction and allows the ski to slide over the surface more easily.

Slip sliding away

Friction occurs when two things slide together. It is a force that slows things down. Imagine pushing a heavy box across the floor. You would feel resistance, and that is friction. There is less friction between smooth things: the box would slide more freely across a wooden floor than on carpet. Skiers slide smoothly and quickly across the snow because the thin film of water puts up less resistance than the crunchy snow.

FACT 96

The dots on a basketball are called pebbles and are there to increase friction between your hand and the ball.

CROSS-COUNTRY SKIS ARE DESIGNED TO BOTH SLIDE AND GRIP ON THE SNOW.

Getting hotter

Sliding things across each other can create heat. That is why you might rub your hands together in cold weather to warm them up. Friction slows things down, and the kinetic energy is transferred into heat energy. Without friction, you wouldn't be able to rub two sticks together to start a fire, or even strike a match. Friction can generate enough heat to burn your skin, such as holding a rope with your bare hands as you slide down.

Friction can explain why your hands hurt in the gym!

FACT 97

If it wasn't for friction, you would find it hard to stand, sit, or even lie in bed without sliding around.

The good...

Friction can be extremely useful, or it can cause problems. The brakes on a bicycle use friction to make it slow down and stop, by pressing a brake pad against the moving wheel. Friction between the ground and the wheels gives better grip on the road to make the bike move, and stop it skidding.

... and the bad

However, friction between the moving parts of a vehicle wastes the energy being provided by the fuel. It can grind away the surface of the parts so they need replacing. Applying a lubricant, such as oil, will reduce the friction and make the engine run more efficiently and smoothly.

FACT 98

A PARACHUTE HAS A HOLE IN IT

Air gathers underneath a parachute to act against gravity. A small hole is needed to help the parachutist stay in control instead of swinging dangerously in the sky.

A smooth descent

Air resistance is a type of friction, where a moving object pushes against the air. You can feel it on your face as you zoom down a hill on a bicycle or ride on a roller coaster. A person falling through the air is subject to gravity, pulling them to Earth. Using a parachute will slow their descent to make it safer. However, the air beneath the parachute ripples around as it tries to find a way out. The hole at the top allows the air to escape evenly, creating a smoother, safer ride.

I hope that hole is meant to be there!

AIR AND WATER RESISTANCE ARE SOMETIMES REFERRED TO AS DRAG.

A motorcyclist leans forward to increase the streamlining of the bike.

That's the point

Air is a combination of gases, all made up of molecules. A moving object has to push these molecules aside to be able to move through them. Some shapes, called **streamlined** shapes, move the molecules more effectively. The pointed nose of a plane is designed to help it fly efficiently. The world's fastest planes, cars, motorcycles, and even cyclists all use streamlining to reduce air resistance and increase their speed.

Falling down

Gravity pulls on all things equally. If you drop a brick and a feather from a tall building, gravity pulls them to Earth at the same rate. However, logic tells you that the brick would hit the ground first. That's because the feather is subject to more air resistance. Its surface fans out and hits more air, slowing it down.

Super swimmers

Water is also made up of molecules, and so creates resistance against moving objects. Competition divers and swimmers create a streamlined shape, with a small surface area, to cut through the water as neatly and efficiently as possible. Nature has many examples of superbly streamlined creatures, from sharks and penguins to dolphins and swordfish. Submarine designers have copied their shapes for their own use.

FACT 99

ASTRONAUTS DON'T SNORE

And they don't burp, either! It's all because their spacecraft is constantly falling and catching up with the pull of gravity. So it seems that there's no gravity on board.

Free passage

You snore because **gravity** pulls down your tongue and the soft tissue in your throat, so they partly block your windpipe Those soft bits vibrate (the snore) each time you breathe, just as a reed in a clarinet vibrates when air passes it. Except most people prefer the sound of a clarinet to a snore! Without gravity to pull those bits down, you don't wind up snoring.

ASTRONAUTS SOMETIMES GO ON A SPACE WALK TO CARRY OUT REPAIRS.

I'm all spaced out...

You can dream of becoming an astronaut; just don't expect to snore!

Testing, testing

Astronauts might be cooped up for months at a time, so it's important that they remain healthy. They're tested beforehand to make sure no problems become serious during a mission. It's also vital that they stay calm and are able to work with others. The bottom line? You'll fly high if you don't get on other people's nerves!

Bubble trouble

Anything that you let go on a spacecraft: peanuts, a crayon, or another astronaut in a sleeping bag, will float and drift around because there seems to be no gravity. Liquids gather in droplets because their molecules are drawn to each other. The outside is like an elastic layer which holds the molecules together in a sphere.

What a gas!

You don't have to worry about burping, either. That's also down to gravity, which is needed to separate gases from liquid in your stomach. Back on Earth, those gases bubble up from the stomach liquid and escape as burps. Without gravity, they stay mixed.

FACT 100 Water doesn't flow in space.

ASTRONAUTS TRAIN IN SWIMMING POOLS TO GET USED TO MOVING AND WORKING IN EXTREME CONDITIONS.

FACT 101

NEPTUNE'S SUMMER LASTS 40 EARTH YEARS

Like Earth, Neptune has different seasons, with more sunlight in the summertime. However, as Neptune takes almost 165 years to go once around the Sun, summer lasts for much, much longer.

Leaning over

Planets have seasons because their axis is slightly tilted. The axis is an invisible line through the middle, from top to bottom. Mercury spins neatly around an upright axis, but several other planets tilt, including Earth and Neptune. In summer, an area is tilted toward the Sun. In winter, it is tilted away from the Sun. On Earth, each hemisphere has four seasons. Places near the Equator do not tip very much, so the weather stays the same all year round.

URANUS IS TILTED SO MUCH IT SPINS ON ITS SIDE, LIKE A BALL ROLLING ALONG THE GROUND!

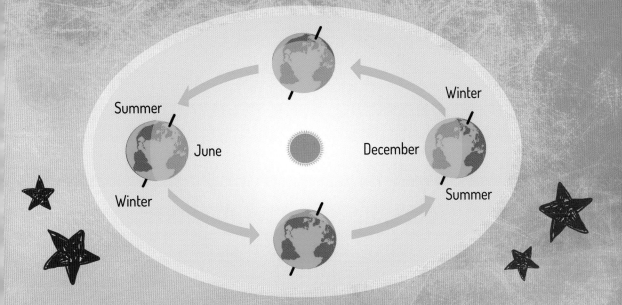

Summer

June

Winter

Winter

December

Summer

How seasons work

Imagine that each planet is an orange with a pin to show your country. If you hold the orange upright, and walk it around a Sun, the pin will always receive the same amount of light. Now tilt the orange slightly. On its next circuit, the pin will point more directly toward the Sun for some of the time, and away from the Sun for the rest of the time. The difference in the amount of sunlight creates different seasons.

Day and night

At the same time as the planets orbit the Sun, each one is rotating (spinning) on its own axis. The pin on your orange moves around, passing from day into night with each rotation. On Earth, this takes roughly 24 hours, but as every planet rotates at a different speed, the length of a day varies greatly. Jupiter has the shortest day of all: less than 10 Earth hours. Venus rotates so slowly that its day is longer than its year!

A DAY ON VENUS LASTS FOR 243 EARTH DAYS WHILE A YEAR LASTS 225 EARTH DAYS.

In orbit

Astronomy, the study of stars, planets, and other items in space, is one of the oldest sciences. In the 1500s a Polish astronomer, Nicolaus Copernicus, presented the theory that the planets **orbit** (circle) around the Sun, and not around the Earth as was previously thought. It was controversial, but it led to many more discoveries about the solar system and the planets in it.

The Sun sets every 24 hours on Earth.

Index